ADVERTISING AND THE FIRST AMENDMENT

A Twentieth Century Fund Paper

ADVERTISING and The First Amendment

by Michael G. Gartner

 Priority Press Publications/New York/1989

The Twentieth Century Fund is a research foundation undertaking timely analyses of economic, political, and social issues. Not-for-profit and non-partisan, the Fund was founded in 1919 and endowed by Edward A. Filene.

Library of Congress Cataloging-in-Publication Data

Gartner, Michael, 1938–
    Advertising and the First Amendment

    "A Twentieth Century Fund paper"
Bibliography: p.
Includes index.
    1. Advertising laws—United States.   2. Freedom of speech—United States.   I. Title.
KF1614.G37   1989   343.73'082   89-3596
ISBN 0-87078-237-1   347.30382
ISBN 0-87078-236-3 (pbk.)

Foreword

Virtually everyone agrees that smoking is bad for you. Each package of cigarettes sold in the United States is required by law to carry one of four dire messages, and Surgeon General C. Everett Koop, a leader in the fight against smoking, recently reported—to the dismay of those who claimed that free choice was at work in their decision to smoke—that smoking is as addictive as cocaine. And yet many Americans continue to smoke and, in many cases, to die. The answer, a growing number believe, is to ban cigarette advertising; they argue that such a ban would, at the very least, help prevent young people from taking up smoking. But others vigorously oppose such an advertising ban, arguing that in an attempt to eradicate one evil, another is encouraged.

What is at issue is commercial speech—the speech of the peddler and the advertiser. Few would dispute the importance of freedom of speech in a democracy, but many question whether commercial speech warrants the same protections as, for example, those given the press.

The Fund has long been interested in the press and, in recent years, in the issue of commercial speech. In 1986, *A Two-Faced Press?* by Tom Goldstein, a Twentieth Century Fund Paper, explored the issue of whether freedom of the press should be extended to a newspaper's advertising columns. The Fund was intrigued by the policy issues Goldstein raised. When Michael G. Gartner proposed another paper, one that would take an opposing view, the Fund couldn't resist adding another voice to the debate.

Gartner believes passionately in the First Amendment and is averse to censorship in all forms and for all reasons. For him, a flourishing democracy and a vital economy rest on an informed public—commercial speech and noncommercial speech are inextricably intertwined. There is something refreshing about Gartner's approach: he neither hedges nor waffles. Whether one ultimately agrees with him is irrelevant. What matters is the clarity of his argument and the manner in which it forces the reader to clarify his own thoughts on this issue. He has done a splendid job, and we are grateful to him for it.

Marcia Bystryn, ACTING DIRECTOR
The Twentieth Century Fund
March 1989

Contents

Acknowledgments

Doris Batliner, the librarian at the *Courier-Journal* in Louisville, Kentucky, laboriously gathered over a period of several months hundreds of documents on commercial speech, ranging from law review articles and unpublished theses to short letters to the editor in obscure publications. David Vestal, a lawyer and journalism student in Iowa City, Iowa, painstakingly organized and catalogued all the material—and, in the process of reading it all, developed his own view that restrictions on commercial speech are necessary and proper. Subsequent discussions with him sharpened my own thinking. He also edited the final version. I am grateful to him and to Ms. Batliner, as well as to Robert Sack, a lawyer who has taught me much and who graciously read this paper in manuscript form.

Preface

Two hundred years after the founding of this nation and nearly two hundred years after the writing of the Bill of Rights, it is taken for granted in this greatest of democracies that speech is free.

A voter can criticize his government.
A sportswriter can castigate the home team.
A politician can ridicule his opponent.
A worker can blow the whistle on his employer.
A churchgoer can question his preacher.
A teacher can tell off the school board.

But:

A lawyer often can't ask an accident victim for his business.
A company can't urge you to buy its stock.
A cigarette maker can't advertise its wares on television.
A liquor seller sometimes can't post his prices.

Speech is free to the voter and the reporter, the politician and the worker, the churchgoer and the teacher, but it is not free to the peddler and the advertiser.

For the peddler and the advertiser deal in commercial speech, and such speech is not accorded all the rights of regular speech. Commercial speech takes many forms—the billboards on the highway, the for-sale sign in the yard, the newsboy hawking newspapers at the stop sign, the "Dear Occupant" letter offering fantastic bargains on land in the Ozarks, the newspaper vending machine in the airport, the placard in the donut-shop window, as well as the everyday advertisements carried by newspapers, television, and radio.

Scores of law review articles and papers have addressed the issue, examining the series of court decisions that, since 1942, have relegated commercial speech to second-class status. It is an issue with many facets, and scholars come down on every side of it.

This paper seeks to explore and explain commercial speech. It does not, however, delve into certain aspects of the subject: false commercial speech, commercial speech and zoning, and so-called time, place, and manner restrictions on commercial speech.

False commercial speech, although an exceedingly important topic, is not examined here because the law and logic in this area are well established. Under the law, false commercial speech can be regulated or prohibited because, as the Supreme Court has stated, the First Amendment does not afford protection to illegal conduct in which speech is incidentally employed. For instance, insider stock tips, presidential death threats, and defamation can all be regulated, even though they involve speech. Likewise, since deception in a commercial transaction constitutes fraud, deceptive speech can be prohibited even though truthful commercial speech is protected.

Here I concentrate on the restrictions imposed by courts and legislatures on the *truthful* advertising of lawful products. I look at the impact of such restrictions on behavior and on freedom, and I arrive at a clear conclusion.

In writing this paper, I examined more than five hundred writings and many, many court cases. I also interviewed numerous lawyers and scholars with expertise in this area of the law.

As a newspaperman and a lawyer and an American, I entered this project with a bias toward freedom of speech for all. I finished the project with an even stronger belief that restrictions on commercial speech are ineffective as social policy and dangerous to our democracy.

Michael G. Gartner
Des Moines, Iowa
July 1988

N.B.: Since completing this manuscript, I have become president of NBC News. I want to make it clear that my proposal to pump dollars into television through government advertising occurred to me before I lined up at the television trough.

Chapter 1
Introduction

In April 1987, the awkwardly named Subcommittee on Transportation, Tourism and Hazardous Materials of the House Committee on Energy and Commerce held hearings on the harm done to us by the smoking of cigarettes. Among those testifying was James S. Todd, a doctor with the unwieldy title of senior deputy executive vice president of the American Medical Association.

"The health consequences of tobacco use have proven to be so serious and so difficult to correct that we cannot afford to overlook *any* preventive measure . . . ," Dr. Todd told the lawmakers. He went on to espouse the idea that the advertising—but not the use—of cigarettes and tobacco should be banned in this country. The position "was not a decision that the AMA took lightly," Dr. Todd told the committee. "We certainly appreciate the First Amendment freedoms we enjoy in this nation."

The American Medical Association does indeed appreciate First Amendment freedoms. Less than a year after Todd made his remarks, in early 1988, the *Journal of the American Medical Association* ran an anonymous letter to the editor in which a young doctor told how he, or maybe she, injected a dying twenty-year-old woman with enough morphine to kill her. ("With clocklike certainty, within four minutes the breathing rate slowed even more, then became irregular, then ceased. . . . It's over, Debbie.")

The dramatic letter caught the attention of the authorities in Chicago, who wondered if perhaps the doctor had committed a murder. The authorities subpoenaed the journal to disclose the name of the doctor.

The AMA refused to talk, arguing that the subpoena interfered with a free press as protected by the First Amendment.

3

I wondered aloud about this in the pages of *The Wall Street Journal*. The American Medical Association, I wrote, seemed to believe that the First Amendment protects those who anonymously want to tell you how they killed somebody, but not those who want to get you to buy a legal product that might cause you to kill yourself. That, I argued, was having it both ways, and you can't do that. You can't appeal to freedoms when it's to your convenience and smother them when it's not.

Kirk Johnson, the general counsel of the AMA, responded in a letter to the editor: "The First Amendment at its heart protects the freedom of the press—including medical journals—and the expression of ideas—even repugnant ones such as those expressed in the AMA Journal story about an act of euthanasia."

He went on: "But commercial speech—the peddler selling his product—historically had no First Amendment protection at all, and the Supreme Court continues to recognize the 'common sense distinction' between commercial advertising and other forms of speech. Thus, the Supreme Court last term upheld a ban on gambling advertising in Puerto Rico even though gambling is lawful there, and a federal ban on tobacco advertising likely would be upheld as well. There is no 'lawful-to-sell, lawful-to-advertise' principle under the First Amendment. . . . The AMA does not take its First Amendment rights, or anybody else's, casually."

But the AMA does take First Amendment rights casually, and it isn't alone. Each year, some $120 billion is spent on advertising in this country, and all those words, all those ideas, all those pitches, all that writing, and all those pictures have only limited protection under the First Amendment. This category of speech—called commercial speech by the courts and lawyers—has only second-class status, at best. Oddly, few people—journalists, advertisers, or legislators—seem to care.

They should, because commercial speech is expression, and freedom of expression is necessary in a democracy. An intelligent, self-governing people must shop freely in the marketplace of ideas, and that marketplace contains commercial as well as political stalls. No stall should be closed by the thought police. "The best test of truth is the power of thought to get itself accepted in the competition of the market," Justice Oliver Wendell Holmes wrote in 1919. Every person must develop his own views and philosophy, and this cannot occur if any expression, any idea, is censored.

Commercial speech is really just an unnecessary and confusing term that lawyers have concocted. When we talk about commercial speech, we are simply talking about the right of businesses truthfully to promote legal products and services in the commercial marketplace without interference from government.

There is no reason—though the AMA, the Supreme Court, the law journals and professors, and legislators have certainly tried to find one—that truthful commercial speech should be suppressed, even a little, in a country where free speech reigns. There is every reason why it should not be suppressed.

What the Founders Thought

The regulation of commercial speech is not just a theoretical problem. In the United States, where "Congress shall make no law abridging the freedom of speech . . . or of the press . . . ," it is perfectly legal to ban advertising for a product or service that itself is perfectly legal. And it is being done.

In the United States today:

• It is illegal to advertise cigarettes or tobacco products on television or radio. The products themselves, of course, are legal.

• It is illegal to mail "any newspaper, circular, pamphlet, or publication of any kind containing any advertising of a lottery or similar enterprise, or any list of prizes awarded in such an enterprise," according to postal regulations. (There is an exception: a newspaper can run advertising about an official lottery in its own or an adjacent state.)

• It is a criminal offense, punishable by a fine of up to $1,000 or imprisonment for a year or both, for any broadcaster knowingly to permit the broadcasting of any ad about lotteries except for official ones run by the state.

• It is illegal to use interstate commerce or the mails—including any writing or broadcast material—to offer any stock or security for sale. All that is permitted are so-called tombstone ads that state where a prospectus for a security can be obtained.

• It is legal for states to regulate the advertising of liquor. And several states do.

• It is legal for states to prohibit lawyers from engaging in in-person solicitation of clients; it is also legal for them to regulate the content of advertising by lawyers.

• It is illegal in Nevada to advertise a brothel in counties where prostitution is illegal even though the brothel itself is operating legally in another county.

• It is illegal in North Dakota for a licensed dealer in pistols to place a placard ad in his window saying that he sells them.
• It is illegal in New Jersey for doctors' ads to contain testimonials from satisfied patients.
• It is illegal in Utah to advertise cigarettes on billboards or buses.
• It is illegal in most instances to display U.S. currency in advertising.
• It is illegal in many states to advertise for surrogate motherhood arrangements.

How did all this come about?

Advertising has been around since at least the days of the founders of this republic. Yet historians have failed to uncover any meaningful discussion of advertising at the time the First Amendment was debated. Did the founders just assume that advertising would be protected? After all, the First Amendment doesn't guarantee "freedom of *noncommercial* speech"; it refers only to freedom of speech, period. Or did the founders just assume that advertising was such a stepchild form of expression that of course it wasn't protected and everyone knew it?

The predominant view is that the First Amendment was an attempt to secure freedom of political, rather than commercial, speech. Judges and philosophers have declared many times over that the First Amendment was a response to colonial prosecutions for seditious libel. Ever since the adoption of the Bill of Rights, it has been widely assumed that the original purpose of the First Amendment was to permit free and open criticism of government.

Thus a judge in 1941 wrote that "such men as Thomas Paine, John Milton and Thomas Jefferson were not fighting for the right to peddle commercial advertising." Similarly, in a dissent to a 1977 advertising case, Justice William Rehnquist wrote: "If those responsible for the Bill of Rights, by feats of valor or efforts at draftsmanship, could have lived to know that their efforts had enshrined in the Courts the right of commercial vendors of contraceptives to peddle those to unmarried minors through such means as window displays and vending machines located in the men's rooms of truck stops, not-withstanding the considered judgment of the New York Legislature to the contrary, it is not difficult to imagine their reaction."

In a Ph.D. thesis for the University of Minnesota in 1977, Kent Richards Middleton attempted to trace the intentions of the founders with respect to commercial speech. Justice Rehnquist might be surprised. Middleton wrote:

The role of commercialism in the eighteenth century as well as intellectual and legal currents of the time offer little conclusive evidence that the founding fathers would have necessarily excluded commercial advertising from First Amendment protections. More persuasive evidence that the First Amendment was never intended to protect commercial speech is the relentless repetition by judges, philosophers and politicians since the eighteenth century of the idea that free expression must be protected for political—not commercial—reasons.

The founding fathers were conspicuously reticent about what the First Amendment was supposed to mean. No American leader is known to have argued specifically for including commercial advertising under the First Amendment, but isolated statements and common ideas of the period provide evidence that advertising might not have been categorically excluded from First Amendment protections. "A free press," Richard Henry Lee said in his demand for a Bill of Rights, "is the channel of communication to *mercantile* and public affairs. . . ." The not-uncommon belief in the eighteenth century that speech should be free ". . . as far as . . . it . . . does not hurt or control the Right of Another . . ." also leaves room for advertising in a theory of protected expression.

Other evidence is found in the extensive use of advertising in the eighteenth century. The 1700s were a time of growing commercialism when advertising was of unquestioned value in announcing the arrival of a new shipload of useful products. After a long wait, a homemaker was often more interested in learning through advertising about the newly imported calicoes than in stale news of foreign intrigue.

The founding fathers, like other citizens in the eighteenth century, were not unfamiliar with, or hostile to, commercial advertising. They were materialistic people, some of whom used advertising themselves. George Washington advertised western lands in the newspaper.

Because the eighteenth century was a period of aggressive, individual commercial efforts, the distinction made by the supreme court in 1942 between editorial content and "purely commercial" advertising may never have occurred to the founding fathers. It was difficult at that time to draw a line between the commercial and the editorial. Advertising did not have a format or position in the paper distinct from news, and the paper's staff was not yet specialized. The editor was often reporter, salesman, editor and book-keeper all at once.

To the scholarly founders, free and open discourse was indispensable if people were to remain informed about important matters. Since economic concerns played a central role in the lives of all Americans—then as now—the framers may have accorded communication of information needed for personal economic decisions a high degree of protection from governmental interference.

"Our framers understood that it makes no difference from the standpoint of free speech and self-government whether information appears in a news column or in a paid advertisement," Bruce Sanford, a lawyer who represents the media, told a business conference in 1987. "Both have value. Both contribute to informed decisionmaking in a free enterprise society."

Setting Limits—Why, and Why Not

So what happened? If indeed the founders believed in free speech for advertising as well as news and politics, how did we get to our sorry current state, in which messages sent to us can be cleared—or even banned—by the state?

What happened is this: over the years, especially in this century, judges and regulators have devised constitutional arguments to limit the protections accorded commercial speech. They are:

1. *Commercial speech bears no relation to public decisionmaking.* Though not exactly a new argument, the idea here is that commercial speech is undeserving of protection because the First Amendment applies only to issues relevant to the political process, to speech concerning how the government should be run. Proponents of this view hold that commercial speech does not contribute to political decisionmaking. A 1987 article in the *University of Toronto Law Journal*, while conceding that advertising may have an impact on political decisions, concluded that "a theory of political expression which included any utterance which has impact upon political decisions would simply sweep in too much to retain coherence."

In a similar vein, an article in the *University of Illinois Law Review* in 1986 argued that "proposals for commercial transactions are so distinct from political debate that any public interest in advertisements is totally irrelevant to first amendment values. Speech which does no more than propose a commercial transaction does not involve any expression essential to self-government."

That, of course, is hogwash. The free-market economy and our democratic system are inseparable. In a democracy, if people are to make their own personal, economic, and intellectual choices, there must be a free exchange of commercial opinion and information. Pure commercial speech may not affect how people are governed as directly as political speech does, but it indirectly affects people's attitudes and values about how they should be governed. While politics can shape a man's business, his business can just as surely shape his politics.

2. *Freedom of expression protects an open exchange of views in order to create a competitive marketplace of ideas, which will in turn enhance the search for truth.* In this view, commercial speech should not be protected because it is just huckstering and is not involved with *ideas.* Since commercial speech is just one company saying its product is better or newer or cheaper or costlier or nicer or prettier than the competition's, it is less integrally involved with ideas and thus not worthy of constitutional protection.

The argument was succinctly stated in the *Virginia Law Review* in 1979: "Measured in terms of traditional First Amendment principles, commercial speech is remarkable for its insignificance."

In truth, commercial speech performs a strong informational function, allowing consumers to make better-informed decisions about allocating their scarce resources. Advertising may be less objective than news copy, but it is no less informative. As Burt Neuborne, a First Amendment authority and professor of law at New York University, said in the summer of 1988, "Even if speech about economic choice was not essential to a functioning economic democracy, it would be entitled to special protection because it is among the most potent conveyors of information and ideas in modern society."

3. *Commercial speech can be regulated because the motivation of the regulators is not based on disapproval of the message.* Those holding this view maintain that the intent of the framers in drafting the First Amendment was to prevent the state from suppressing speech it disfavored. Commercial speech is regulated out of concern for public health and welfare, not out of any intolerance for ideas. Therefore, regulation of commercial speech does not violate the First Amendment.

This is a slick argument, but it is not true. In fact, most regulation of truthful commercial speech springs from the distaste of regulators or the courts for the message transmitted. Recent history abounds with prohibitions on ads for activities that, though legal, were thought to threaten the community's moral standards. Nevada, which has legalized prostitution, prohibits brothels from advertising on public streets or highways or in any place of business. Puerto Rico attempts to discourage residents from engaging in legal casino gambling by forbidding advertising on the island. Likewise, many states prohibit ads for surrogate motherhood arrangements, even though the practice itself is legal.

4. *The protection of commercial speech cheapens or dilutes the constitutional protection afforded other speech.* Former Justice Potter Stewart noted in the Pentagon Papers case that when everything is classified, nothing is. In the same way, say those in this camp, protecting all speech equally means protecting no speech at all. As the U.S. Supreme Court said in a unanimous 1978 opinion in the case of *Ohralik v. Ohio State Bar Association,* "To require a parity of constitutional protection for commercial and non-commercial speech alike could invite dilution, simply by a leveling process, of the force of the Amendment's guarantee with respect to the latter kind of speech."

Chief Justice Rehnquist has persistently argued this point, maintaining that the First Amendment, "long regarded by the Court as a sanctuary for expressions of public importance or intellectual interest, is demeaned by invocation to protect advertising of goods and services." He added, "advertising, however truthful or reasonable it may be, is not the sort of expression that the First Amendment was adopted to protect."

But if the speech is protected by the First Amendment, as commercial speech is, that should be the end of the debate. The level of protection should not vary according to the value members of the public might accord that speech. For who is to determine the scale of values? The Constitution does not establish a class of philosopher-kings to decide for all of us which forms of speech, among all those protected by the First Amendment, deserve more protection and which less.

The First Amendment mentions only one classification of speech: *free.* Yet judges believe that they and other government officials have the right to police commercial speech in a way they never would dream of doing if noncommercial speech were involved.

5. *Commercial speech should be regulated because its purveyors are very knowledgeable about their subject and thus must be held to a higher standard than those engaging in other forms of speech.* In the words of former Justice Lewis Powell: "Two features of commercial speech

permit regulation of its content. First, commercial speakers have extensive knowledge of both the market and their products. Thus they are well-situated to evaluate the accuracy of their messages and the lawfulness of the underlying activity. In addition, commercial speech, the offspring of economic self-interest, is a hardy breed of expression that is not particularly susceptible to being crushed by overbroad regulation."

This is tantamount to saying that speech in general should be protected because the speakers often don't know what they're talking about and thus should be free to say whatever wild things pop into their minds. As for thoughtful, sound ideas on commercial topics, well, these need not be protected.

Chapter 2
Legally Speaking

For 150 years, the regulation of commercial speech was not much of an issue in America. The press—and, certainly, advertisers—was strong and robust, and there was little movement to regulate content of any sort. As far as the press was concerned, "the First Amendment was in essence a dead letter—it wasn't really needed—until the 1930s," notes Robert Sack, a partner in the New York office of Gibson, Dunn & Crutcher and a First Amendment author, scholar, and litigator. "It was just there in the Constitution, the way 'We the people' is there. The general understanding was that the press could say anything it wanted to." A look at advertisements of the last century—the miracle cure-alls, snake-oil pitches, and the like—indicates that commercial speech was as free and robust and wild as political speech.

During the nineteenth and early twentieth centuries, government regulation of the press was all but nonexistent. "An easy and uncontested freedom of speech and of the press prevailed throughout the nineteenth century," Alexander Bickel noted. "During this period the First Amendment was legally an unquestioned assumption."

It was not until 1919, when the Bill of Rights was 128 years old, that the first freedom-of-speech case reached the Supreme Court. The question of First Amendment rights for commercial speech was not addressed by the Supreme Court until 1942. That initial case, *Valentine v. Chrestensen,* dealt with a Sanitary Code ordinance in New York City that regulated the distribution of handbills containing "purely commercial advertising." A man named Chrestensen owned a former U.S. Navy submarine and sold tickets for tours of it. He advertised the tours on a handbill but was told that such advertising couldn't be distributed on the streets of New York. He then added to the handbills some editorial criticism of the City Dock Department for refusing him wharfage facilities. This editorial matter, he reasoned, took the handbill out of the realm of commercial speech. The New York courts agreed with him.

The Supreme Court disagreed. In a unanimous opinion, the court held that the editorial material was added only to get around the law. In a four-page opinion, the Court invented the doctrine that commercial speech— "purely commercial advertising"—is not protected by the First Amendment. The Court itself ruled only on handbills, but other courts and lawmakers broadened the doctrine's application, and before long it was established law in this land of the free that advertisers basically had no rights under the First Amendment.

And thus was born one of the most oppressive and undemocratic doctrines of our time. In the 1950s, 1960s, and 1970s it came to be used by consumerists, regulators, and legislators greatly to restrict our freedom of speech and our freedom to learn and debate. Since 1942 the degree of suppression of commercial speech has ebbed and flowed—in some years the courts have been more hostile than in others—but the suppression continues to this day. In fact, today the controls on commercial speech are tighter than they were a decade ago, and, like the suppression of civil rights of blacks in America, they remain an outrage to democracy.

The doctrine enunciated in Chrestensen was not reexamined by the Supreme Court until 1973. Then, ruling on a Pittsburgh ordinance forbidding newspapers to run help-wanted ads that were segregated by sex (help wanted/male; help wanted/female), the Court again held that truthful commercial speech was not entitled to protection under the First Amendment. Referring to the 1942 Chrestensen case, the Court distinguished between unprotected advertisements that do "no more than propose a commercial transaction" and those ads that express a position on matters of social or political policy and are therefore protected by the First Amendment. It was the second of many attempts to regulate truthful commercial speech, attempts that have led to a maze of state and federal laws, court decisions, and regulations, a maze that was unneeded, unwise, and, in the view of many, unconstitutional.

As the court cases and legislation proliferated, some rules were established. In 1975, the Supreme Court ruled in *Bigelow v. Virginia* that in deciding commercial-speech cases a court "may not escape the task of assessing the First Amendment interest at stake and weighing it against the public interest allegedly served by the regulations."

The next year, 1976, the Court began backing away from stringent controls on commercial speech. Rejecting the balance test put forward just a year earlier, Justice Harry Blackmun, writing for the majority, stated in *Virginia State Board of Pharmacy v. Virginia Citizens Consumer Council:* "It is precisely this kind of choice, between the danger of suppressing information, and the dangers of its misuse if it is freely available, that the First Amendment makes for us."

But the Court that giveth can also taketh away, and the *Virginia Pharmacy* decision contained a qualifying footnote that was of lasting importance. It stated that commercial speech, though protected by the First Amendment, does not qualify for the same rights as political speech. "There are commonsense differences between speech that does no more than propose a commercial transaction and other varieties," the footnote asserted. "Even if the differences do not justify the conclusion that commercial speech is valueless, and thus subject to complete suppression by the State, they nonetheless suggest that *a different degree of protection is necessary to insure that the flow of truthful and legitimate commercial information is unimpaired*" (emphasis added).

This assertion of a "commonsense difference" between commercial and political speech has been quoted for years; it has never been adequately explained.

Four years later, in 1980, the Supreme Court elaborated on its views of commercial speech in *Central Hudson Gas & Electric Corp. v. Public Service Commission of New York*. In striking down a New York State ban on promotional advertising by electric utilities, the Court developed a four-part test to determine if restraint could be imposed on commercial speech. The test:

1. The speech must concern lawful activity and not be misleading.
2. The proposed ban must involve a substantial governmental interest.
3. The proposed ban must directly advance the governmental interest.
4. The proposed ban must be no more extensive than necessary to serve that interest.

All of this was not just theoretical. The four-part test came about at a time when consumerism was at its height. The Reagan years had not yet begun, and regulation, not deregulation, was the wave. Ever since the election of Lyndon Johnson in 1964, increasing pressures from the consumer movement and government had given rise "to all kinds of desires to protect the public health through control of advertising," notes Robert Sack. "In the 1940s, it was not widely thought to be the government's responsibility to censor cigarette ads about 'protecting your T-zone.' When it came to advertising, this was much more of a laissez-faire society."

By 1980, however, when the four-part test was devised, the nation was full of courts and legislatures wanting to restrict advertising. The four-part test became a yardstick to measure freedom—and a pillow to burke it. The *Central Hudson* case provided "an analytical framework under which even truthful promotions of lawful products may constitutionally be restricted," noted James Mercurio, a Washington lawyer. In so doing, the Court "legitimized a degree of regulation of nonmisleading commercial speech that would be anathema in any other area of First Amendment jurisprudence," a *Columbia Law Review* article observed in 1982.

Commercial speech was first protected from regulation in 1976, but only four years later the *Central Hudson* Court took away a large measure of that protection.

The next blow came in 1986, when the Court ruled on *Posadas De Puerto Rico Associates v. Tourism Company of Puerto Rico.* A new conservative majority retreated from, but did not overrule, the *Virginia Pharmacy* case, and in the process took a giant step back toward stiff regulation of commercial speech.

Thus, even as Ronald Reagan and his followers were deregulating America, the Supreme Court, with the help of Reagan's appointees, was re-regulating commercial speech. While Reagan appointees to government agencies generally would free, or at least ease, the rules and regulations on commercial speech, his appointees to the Supreme Court, and especially his choice as Chief Justice, William Rehnquist, have spearheaded the effort to muzzle free speech in the commercial marketplace.

The 1986 *Posadas* case involved a ban in Puerto Rico on the advertising of legal casino gambling. It reflected the Puerto Rican government's effort to discourage island residents—as opposed to tourists—from gambling. In what Professor Philip Kurland called a "dreary exercise in small-town authoritarianism," Puerto Rico officials argued that casino gambling by residents "would produce serious harmful effects on the health, safety and welfare of the Puerto Rican citizens," including the "disruption of moral and cultural patterns, the increase in local crime, the fostering of prostitution, the development of corruption and the infiltration of organized crime." Under the Puerto Rican law, ads aimed at others—predominantly tourists—must first be cleared by the commonwealth.

In a five-to-four vote, the Court upheld the advertising ban, holding that because gambling was not a constitutionally protected activity, and because the government had the power to ban gambling, it also had the "lesser" power to ban gambling advertising. Writing for the majority (and using very emphatic language), Chief Justice Rehnquist rejected the argument that Puerto Rico could not suppress speech about a legal product or service: "In our view, appellant has the argument backwards. . . . (I)t is precisely *because* the government could have enacted a wholesale prohibition of the underlying conduct that it is permissible for the government to take the less intrusive step of allowing the conduct, but reducing the demand through restrictions on advertising."

Such reasoning seems highly illogical. Since very few products or services are constitutionally protected, the Court's decision essentially invests the government with the power to ban advertising for almost anything. "Companies subject to worker-protection regulations or products-liability laws, or licenses and permit requirements of any form, apparently won't be safe from the decision's grip, if the court's logic is carried to its limits," Steven A. Meyerowitz, a writer and lawyer, wrote in *Business Marketing* magazine. The *Los Angeles Times* put it more succinctly in a July 4, 1986, editorial: "If we may be blunt, this notion seems screwy."

Surprisingly, the Reagan administration's reaction to the decision was highly negative. "A good case can be made that Posadas was wrongly decided," a Justice Department official told Congress in 1987. The Court "fundamentally confuses the government's power to regulate behavior with government's absence of—or at least far less—authority to control speech."

First Amendment lawyer Floyd Abrams, writing in the *National Law Journal*, declared that advertisers' defeat in the case was so total "that the question of whether any protection realistically remains for commercial speech must be raised anew."

"A more obvious form of prior restraint is difficult to imagine," Justice John Paul Stevens wrote in a dissent. Separately, Justice William Brennan wrote, "I see no reason why commercial speech should be afforded less protection than other types of speech where, as here, the government seeks to suppress commercial speech in order to deprive consumers of accurate information concerning a lawful activity."

It was a terrible decision, and it has terrible ramifications.

Posadas is a troubling departure from the fundamental principles of commercial speech. While the Court retained the four-part test developed in *Central Hudson*, its conclusion in *Posadas* makes it possible to prohibit completely any commercial speech that is not derived from an underlying constitutional activity. The Court's holding, and its decision to afford legislatures great latitude in applying it, has made commercial speech fair game for regulators.

Chapter 3
Defining the Animal

The *Posadas* decision is especially screwy because there is one type of commercial speech that—at least for now—is considered fully protected by the First Amendment. This is commercial speech that contains a so-called political element.

The distinction is a blurry one at best. The issue was raised by Justice Brennan in a case relating to the regulation of billboards. He wrote that he would be unhappy to see city officials forced to decide whether each of the following billboards constituted political or commercial speech: "the first billboard contains the message 'Visit Joe's Ice Cream Shoppe'; the second, 'Joe's Ice Cream Shoppe uses only the highest quality dairy products'; the third, 'Because Joe thinks that dairy products are good for you, please shop at Joe's Shoppe'; and the fourth, 'Joe says to support dairy price supports: they mean lower prices for you at his Shoppe.'" As Justice Brennan pointed out, it is inconsistent and illogical for one type of commercial speech to be protected while another is not. It's impossible to distinguish political from nonpolitical speech.

In 1983, the Supreme Court for the first time directly addressed the defining characteristics of commercial speech in *Bolger v. Youngs Drugs Product Corps*. The case arose when Youngs distributed three informational pamphlets about condoms through the mails in violation of a federal statute that denied access to the mails to "any unsolicited advertisement of matter . . . designed, adapted or intended to prevent conception. . . ."

The threshold question, ruled the Court, was whether this constituted commercial speech. If so, then content-based restrictions, such as the federal statute Youngs was challenging, were permissible. If, on the other hand, the pamphlets were political speech, said the Court, they were fully protected by the Constitution and not subject to government regulation.

The pamphlet that presented the closest question, "Plain Talk about Venereal Disease," consisted of a general discussion of the problems of venereal disease and the advantages of using condoms to prevent it. Although the pamphlet discussed condoms and condom use, it did not mention brand names. Only at the very bottom of the back page was Youngs identified as the distributor of Trojan-brand condoms.

Was this political speech or commercial speech? The Court said it was the latter, with Justice Thurgood Marshall writing for the majority that "advertising which links a product to a current public debate is not thereby entitled to the constitutional protection afforded noncommercial speech."

A Federal Trade Commission (FTC) administrative law judge ruled differently in a 1986 case involving the R. J. Reynolds Tobacco Company. Reynolds had run an ad entitled "Of Cigarettes and Science." Drafted to resemble an op-ed piece, the ad did not include the name of any particular brand of cigarettes or ask the consumer to buy any particular product. Instead, it discounted the scientific evidence linking cigarette smoking to cardiovascular disease.

The FTC filed a complaint against Reynolds, claiming that the ad was false and misleading commercial speech because of Reynolds's interpretation of the scientific data. Reynolds responded that "Of Cigarettes and Science" was not commercial speech and therefore not subject to government regulation, even if it was false and misleading. The judge in *In Re R. J. Reynolds Tobacco Co.* agreed with Reynolds and dismissed the complaint. The Reynolds advertisement, he wrote, "does not name any brand name or list prices or discuss desirable attributes of a product or show where the product may be purchased." Rather, he said, the advertisement was an editorial expressing Reynolds's point of view in the raging controversy over smoking. And he found that the advertisement does not lose the protection of the First Amendment simply because that view coincides with the company's economic interests.

Oddly, *The New York Times*, that great beneficiary of uninhibited, robust, and wide-open debate, editorialized against the decision. "The issue to be decided here is factual, not constitutional," the *Times* wrote. "Heaven forfend laws to prevent a cosmetics manufacturer from contending that a new lipstick will change a woman's life or a new aftershave a man's. But in law and decency, scientific findings should have to be rendered scrupulously, particularly in matters of life and death."

Decency, maybe, but not law. "Rendered scrupulously" is not part of the First Amendment.

The New York Times, of course, can reject ads it considers not factual, just as it can reject articles from its reporters or free-lancers that it considers insufficiently documented. But it's unlikely that the *Times* would support a ruling requiring its news content to be factual and subjecting it to fact-checking scrutiny by a government hearing examiner.

In 1988, the full Federal Trade Commission came around to the view of the *Times*, reversing its own agency judge. These differing verdicts demonstrate that the line dividing ads of opinion from other ads is so blurred that it is difficult to know in advance whether a given ad falls into one category or the other.

Even if such distinctions were possible, advertisers could certainly recast their messages in ideological terms and obscure the line. Nuclear power companies could promote themselves as "working to develop energy for a strong America" and offering an alternative to foreign oil dependence, while manufacturers of artificial furs could promote their products as an alternative to endangered fur-bearing mammals. In the same way, advertisers for any good or service could compare the relative merits of their product as it affects the economy, the environment, or the general public welfare. As the Supreme Court pointed out in the 1976 *Virginia Pharmacy* case, "Obviously, not all commercial messages contain the same or even a very great public interest element. There are few to which such an element, however, could not be added. . . ."

In reality, the categories of commercial and noncommercial speech cannot be separated. As New York Court of Appeals Judge Jacob Fuchsberg wrote in the *Brooklyn Law Review* in 1980, "as untroubling as neat distinctions between the dissemination of ideas and the distribution of goods may have been in an earlier age, they are well-nigh impossible today."

Picture this: A man is shown riding a bicycle, pedaling merrily along and enjoying the rustic scenery and lovely weather. He is passed by a man in a chauffeur-driven Cadillac, talking on his cellular phone, reading his *Wall Street Journal*, and barking orders to his harried secretary. The ad says: "Live Longer. Buy a Schwinn instead of a Cadillac."

This hypothetical ad is as much a political statement as a pitch for Schwinn bicycles. Should it not be given the same protection as an editorial urging harried executives to slow down, enjoy the scenery, and spend some time tossing a ball with youngsters? Of course it should. But it isn't.

Speech, Free and Indivisible

Commercial speech and political speech cannot be separated. But one can go further: All commercial speech *is* political speech by its very nature. No commercial speech is entirely devoid of noncommercial, political, or social implications.

According to conventional wisdom, the First Amendment exists to ensure a representative form of government; further, the primary purpose of free speech is to allow a free flow of information upon which private citizens can base their political decisions. Given this, critics ask, why is advertising, which says "I will sell you X widget at Y price," entitled to First Amendment protection?

The Supreme Court provided the answer in *Virginia Pharmacy* in 1976. That case, which established limited protection for commercial speech, involved a state law that declared it to be unprofessional for a licensed pharmacist to advertise the price of prescription drugs. The Court said that advertising contributes to enlightened public decisionmaking in a democracy. Not only is the free flow of economic information "indispensable" to the private economic decisions that make the free-market economy work, wrote Justice Blackmun, but it is also "indispensable to the formulation of intelligent opinions as to how that system ought to be regulated or altered. Therefore, even if the First Amendment were thought to be primarily an instrument to enlighten public decisionmaking in a democracy, we could not say that the free flow of information does not serve that goal."

The Court held that the unrestricted flow of information is just as important in the commercial as in the political context. Because commercial speech informs people of the availability of products and services, it facilitates the rational decisionmaking that fosters self-government.

Commercial speech is protected because it fosters informed decisionmaking among consumers. It maximizes the flow of truthful information to consumers so that they can make realistic choices as to their needs. And those choices are important. In fact, as Barbara Burnett of Syracuse Law School has suggested, "to some, the importance of the decisionmaking process is as great in the choice of an automobile as in the choice of a mayor."

Commercial speech is as useful in the marketplace of commercial ideas as political speech is in the arena of political ideas. And both the commercial and political marketplaces are essential to a democracy. It follows, then, that both marketplaces should encourage and embrace free speech. "Some freedom of commercial speech and activity is more than desirable; it is necessary to political democracy, an essential attribute without which the system is jeopardized," the *Ottawa Law Review* stated.

This view was shared by Justice William O. Douglas, who wrote in a 1971 opinion that "the language of the First Amendment does not except speech directed at private economic decisionmaking. Certainly such speech could not be regarded as less important than political expression. When immersed in a free flow of commercial information, private sector decisionmaking is at least as effective an institution as are our various governments in furthering the social interests in obtaining the best general allocation of resources."

After all, who can say for sure whether advertisements with the messages "Going Out of Business," or "Buy Now, Prices Going Up," or "Buy American, Buy Chevy," or even "Gas $3.50 a gallon" present us with a political message or a commercial message? Who knows whether American car ads influence consumer views on foreign-car import restrictions? All information about the quality and price of products potentially relates to important political issues. In our complex society, all issues that affect attitudes about access to needed goods and services are political issues. Economics is politics. Politics is economics.

America is not just a political democracy; it is an economic democracy as well. You needn't buy a particular type of car any more than you need vote for a specific candidate. You needn't wear a specific type of watch any more than you need attend a certain church. Yet we can speak freely within this political democracy and not within the economic democracy.

"Since commercial messages necessarily contain social and political implications, they possess the same potential as other forms of speech to challenge those in political power and constitute a portion of the public dialogue on policy issues," an article in the *Harvard Law Review* noted in 1980. "Because commercial expression furthers the same values and interests that require protection of other forms of speech," the content "should receive full constitutional protection."

In other words, when it comes to the First Amendment, there's no meaningful distinction between commercial speech and political speech.

Disserving the Public

Based on constitutional principles, commercial speech deserves First Amendment protection; in fact, it is exactly the sort of speech that the First Amendment was designed to protect. Aside from legal questions, the regulation of commercial speech makes for bad public policy. For one thing, the second-class status afforded commercial speech means that today every power around—big business, big government, big anything—knows that commercial speech is an easy target.

One Christmas, Anheuser-Busch began stocking store shelves in Ohio with beer cartons featuring the famous mascot Spuds Mackenzie dressed in a Santa Claus outfit and carrying a sack stuffed with Bud Light. The company was soon informed by the Ohio Department of Liquor Control that the cartons ran afoul of an Ohio law preventing the use of Santa Claus to promote alcoholic beverages. The case ended up before the Ohio Liquor Commission, which agreed that the beer company had violated the state law.

An Anheuser-Busch attorney told the *National Law Journal* that the case "had the aspect of comic opera about it." But there is nothing comic about such an assault on commercial speech. The point isn't that one beer company was barred from running one ad. It's that all commercial speech has so little protection in America that courts and legislatures feel completely free to censor advertising about any subject they deem undesirable. The whole idea is repugnant to democracy.

The irony is that while judges and legislators are "protecting" consumers from advertising, consumers seem just as eager to get commercial information as marketers and manufacturers are to provide it. "It is my contention that the force of the argument that commercial speech should be protected . . . comes from a recognition of the interests of the listener rather than those of the speaker," says Robert Sharpe, a Toronto law professor.

In fact, the First Amendment has historically protected the interests of both speaker and listener. I have a right to espouse my views; you have a right to hear them. You have a right to expose my flaws; he has a right to read that. He has a right to extol his cars; we have a right to hear it. Indeed, the 1976 *Virginia Pharmacy* case grew out of a challenge to a state law banning the advertising of prescription drug prices—a challenge that came not from a pharmacist but from a consumers group. The group wanted to know the actual cost of the drugs in order to combat the high overhead costs being imposed by pharmacies. In attempting to justify the ban, proponents argued that price advertising would induce commercialization and that the hustle of the marketplace would negatively affect the delivery of services.

Opponents of the ban, who eventually prevailed, responded that its true purpose was to keep consumers ignorant and thereby discourage competition. They claimed it constituted a sub rosa attempt by the state legislature to subsidize smaller, less efficient pharmacies.

Bans have been used in the past to allow a favored group to maintain artificially high prices and provide haphazard service. The bans have effectively insulated these groups from competition. One example is legal advertising. Measures that prohibit it, while ostensibly designed to assure high professional standards, operate as price-fixing schemes that eliminate the possibility of real competition.

Even well-intentioned restrictions that seek to protect the public—such as the prohibition against cigarette ads on television—are highly paternalistic, underestimating the public's ability to recognize the limits of advertising.

The consuming public wants commercial information. As the Supreme Court recognized in *Virginia Pharmacy*, the authorities, instead of screening the information that the public can receive, should "assume that this information is not in itself harmful, that people will perceive their own best interests if only they are well enough informed, and that the best means to that end is to open the channels of communication rather than to close them."

The public always benefits from an uninhibited, wide-open, and robust—but truthful—debate about any product or service. The best answer is always more speech rather than more regulation. And that's true whether the subject is prescription drugs, smoking, gambling, condoms, or anything else.

Chapter 4
Dealing with Danger

Nowhere is the commercial-speech fight more pronounced than in the continuing battle to ban the advertising of cigarettes.

Virtually everyone except the Tobacco Institute and some tobacco-state legislators agrees that cigarettes kill people. The government believes this. Doctors believe this. Most citizens believe it. Yet virtually everyone agrees, too, that it would be all but impossible to ban the sale of cigarettes. Smoking is as addictive as cocaine, according to Surgeon General C. Everett Koop. A ban on the sale of cigarettes would just create a new illegal industry—the manufacture and sale, underground and without tax revenue, of cigarettes. In effect, we'd just be creating another drug problem.

The answer, say an increasing number of people, is to ban cigarette advertising. This would discourage young people—especially young women, who seem particularly susceptible to cigarette advertising (more girls than boys smoke)—from taking up smoking. The statistics are frightening: although total consumption of cigarettes has declined from its peak in 1981, the annual death toll from cigarettes alone, says Dr. Bob McAfee of the American Medical Association, is still greater than the annual combined number of deaths from heroin, cocaine, alcohol, fire, automobiles, homicide, suicide, and AIDS.

Proponents of an ad ban maintain that the precedent for such a step already exists in the 1971 measure prohibiting the advertising of cigarettes and other products on television.

Indeed, the effort to control smoking in this country goes back even further than that, to 1964, when Luther L. Terry, then the Surgeon General of the Public Health Service, came forth with a report calling cigarettes "a health hazard of sufficient importance . . . to warrant appropriate remedial action." A year later, Congress passed a law requiring that all cigarette packages carry a modest warning: "Caution: Cigarette Smoking May Be Hazardous to Your Health." The tobacco industry, ever one to bargain, agreed to the legislation, purportedly because it put off for several years a proposed ruling from the Federal Trade Commission that would have required the health warnings not only on cigarette packages but in cigarette ads as well.

Four years later, in 1969, Congress toughened the warning to read, "Warning: The Surgeon General Has Determined that Cigarette Smoking Is Dangerous to Your Health." That legislation also was supported by the tobacco industry, apparently because the new law would preempt states and localities that were considering implementing their own bans on cigarette advertising.

That 1969 law, called the Public Health Cigarette Smoking Act, also banned all cigarette advertising in broadcasting after January 1, 1971. "Congress was able to pass the measure without substantial challenges on constitutional grounds because broadcasting uses the public airwaves and generally has not been accorded the same constitutional protections as magazines and newspapers," *The New York Times* noted. (The ban was challenged in *Capital Broadcasting v. Mitchell*, but the Supreme Court upheld it, without comment.)

In 1984, Congress again strengthened the cigarette-pack warning and, for the first time, required that the warnings be included in advertisements. The warnings, which deliver any of four dire messages, are also bigger—by law, of course—than the previous warnings.

Few people seriously argue—though a serious argument could be made—that any of these congressional actions—other than the outright ban of tobacco ads on radio and television—represents an infringement on commercial speech. Regulation of the content of advertising, including requirements that ingredients be listed on labels and that warnings be prominent, is well established.

But banning a whole category of advertising seems extreme. "There is no reason why government should burden First Amendment rights to achieve indirectly what it does not have the courage to achieve directly," Gregory T. Wuliger, a professor of journalism in California, wrote in the *Federal Communications Law Journal*. "If products of any kind are dangerous to the public, it is the product—and not speech about the product—that should be banned."

That view, though, is becoming increasingly scarce. Rep. Mike Synar, an Oklahoma Democrat, has taken the lead in Congress in seeking to ban all advertising of cigarettes for the simple reason that cigarettes kill people. He has some powerful support, most notably from the American Medical Association. Citing the *Posadas* case, the AMA, Rep. Synar, and other proponents see no constitutional barriers to adopting a ban.

But an advertising ban has strong opponents as well. The American Bar Association refuses to endorse it, while both the American Newspaper Publishers Association and the American Civil Liberties Union strongly oppose it; the Reagan administration called it "an exercise in thought control antagonistic to the democratic process." Nonetheless, it seems increasingly likely that a ban, or at least further restrictions, will eventually pass.

All types of schemes abound. In 1986, the American Cancer Society, as "a first step," called for the elimination of all models and scenery in cigarette advertising. It asserted that "advertising copy should merely feature the tar and nicotine content of the product, one of the four rotating warning messages from the Surgeon General, and the price of the product."

Noting this, Tom Goldstein, a lawyer, newspaper reporter, journalism professor, and sometime politician, suggested that one way to regulate cigarette consumption would be to limit ads to ironically named tombstone advertisements, such as those used to advertise stocks and bonds. "Tombstone advertisements," Goldstein noted in a Twentieth Century Fund Paper, *A Two-Faced Press?,* "would eliminate many of the misgivings about advertising that the FTC expressed to Congress in its report on cigarette advertising in the summer of 1985." The FTC complained about ads "designed to imply a relationship between smoking and healthy living by using sports and outdoor activities."

It was precisely such an ad that prompted a federal jury in Newark, New Jersey, to award $400,000 to the widower of Rose Cippollone, a victim of lung cancer. "Just what the doctor ordered," said the ad for L&M cigarettes, which Mrs. Cippollone smoked. "Play Safe—Smoke Chesterfields," said the ad for Chesterfields, which she also smoked. Before Mrs. Cippollone died, she gave a deposition in which she stated that she had paid attention to cigarette advertising and that "through advertising I was led to assume they [the cigarettes] were safe and they wouldn't harm me."

The decision in that case, delivered in June 1988, represented the tobacco industry's first loss after a string of almost three hundred victories over thirty years. Hundreds of more suits are sure to follow. "We are going to file suits from Anchorage to Miami, from Portland, Maine, to San Diego," Melvin Belli, the noted San Francisco trial lawyer, said the day after the decision was announced. "We have been moving slowly over the years, but this one will make all the rest of them easy."

Such suits will no doubt encourage those seeking tougher restrictions on cigarette advertising. In fact, the jurors in Newark were barely home before the politicians began firing. In an interview with *USA Today*, Henry A. Waxman, a California Democrat who is chairman of the health and environment subcommittee of the House Commerce Committee, said: "We're considering a bill right now that would prohibit completely the advertising and promotion of cigarettes. I'm for that bill. . . . It's an important piece of legislation so that we don't leave ourselves vulnerable to the billions of dollars spent each year by the tobacco industry, which ensnares more people into the habit."

All kinds of people are climbing aboard, for all kinds of reasons. Margaret Kriz, a columnist for the *National Journal*, a sober-sided magazine that looks at important issues in America, likened restrictions on cigarette advertising to a *loosening* of restrictions on advertisements for condoms. Condom ads, she wrote, are being accepted in light of public concern over the spread of AIDS, with print and broadcast executives beginning to ease the cultural prohibitions that they had traditionally imposed on themselves. "If it's permissible to tread on social mores in the name of trying to prevent AIDS," Kriz wrote, "is it likewise permissible to curb a free exchange of ideas in the name of stopping deaths attributed to smoking? And after the public is taught that unprotected sex and smoking may be deadly, how much further should the government go?" The two issues have been bound by different restrictions, she noted—one social, the other regulatory. "Both lines should be crossed carefully and infrequently," she wrote, "*but on occasion, cross we must.*"

For More Advertising, Not Less

The reasoning seems backward. If advertising can be used to deal with one social issue, why shouldn't it be used to deal with another? In fact, advertising has proved to be the single most potent weapon in persuading people to quit smoking or to refrain from starting. In 1967, the Federal Communications Commission ruled that the so-called Fairness Doctrine applied to cigarette advertising, meaning that it was a controversial issue of such public importance that broadcasters had to donate time to opponents of smoking. The main opponent was an antismoking group called Action on Smoking and Health, or ASH, headed by an energetic lawyer named John F. Banzhaf III. The FCC ruling was upheld in 1968 by the United States Court of Appeals in Washington.

As a result, the airwaves soon began carrying messages about the perils of smoking and the relationship of smoking to lung cancer. Even though only one antismoking ad was aired for every four cigarette commercials, the message clearly got through. The consumption of cigarettes *declined*, and several surveys indicated that antismoking ads were a major reason. It was for this reason, and this reason alone, that the tobacco companies readily yielded to the 1971 ban on cigarette commercials. For the ban eliminated not only the cigarette commercials but also the antismoking ads—the only really effective weapon ever devised against smoking. After the ban, the tobacco industry simply shifted its ad dollars to print media, which, being an unregulated industry, were not subject to any "fairness" doctrine, so effective antismoking advertising virtually disappeared. As soon as the antismoking ads were stopped, cigarette consumption again began climbing.

The experience proves the wisdom of First Amendment lawyer Robert Sack. Testifying before the House committee considering whether to outlaw cigarette advertising, Sack said: "I would suggest that First Amendment principles here as strongly tell us *what should be done as well as what cannot be*. It is our constitutional faith that, when we face a national problem, what is required is more speech rather than less. . . . If ever more speech rather than less were needed, it is on the consequences of tobacco use."

Indeed, the antismoking commercials, coupled with the reasoning outlined by Sack, suggest that there is a way of reconciling the need to protect our health with the need to protect our rights. The solution: Allow cigarette commercials back on the airwaves. Then have the government produce antismoking commercials and *buy* time to air them on radio and television stations throughout the land. The commercials could be financed by adding a tax on the sale of cigarettes. A two-cents-a-pack tax would produce $575 million annually. That sum admittedly is far less than the $2.5 billion the six cigarette companies spend annually on advertising and promoting their 250 brands, but it's enough to purchase considerably more than the 1,560 antismoking commercials that aired in 1970. (Why buy the ads rather than require they be given free time? The government shouldn't be able to require any private company to give away its products or services, and broadcasting is no different from newspaper or magazine publishing or, for this purpose, steelmaking.)

The proposal would work. District Court Judge Skelly Wright, dissenting in *Capital Broadcasting Co. v. Mitchell*, pointed out that tobacco companies welcomed the ban on cigarette ads because antismoking messages had resulted in a sustained downward trend in cigarette consumption. Indeed, tobacco consumption peaked in 1967, then began to drop in 1968 as the antismoking ads came on the air. Consumption began to rise again when the antismoking ads disappeared from the air. According to Judge Wright, with "the cigarette smoking controversy removed from the air, the decline in cigarette smoking was abruptly halted and cigarette smoking turned upward again." The U.S. experience illustrates that the cure for tobacco advertising is counteradvertising.

The proposal would break no new ground. The government already is a major advertiser, plugging, among other things, the wonderful life in the Army, Navy, Air Force, and Marines. The government has long had the power to tax cigarettes, of course, and it already earmarks some tax receipts for spending on related activities; the gasoline tax, for instance, goes into the highway fund.

The proposal thus presents no constitutional issues, no revenue issues, and no ideological issues; it is merely an extension of the battle between the government and free enterprise, a battle that takes place daily in such arenas as taxes, regulation, and tariffs.

Most important, the proposal avoids that first step down the terrible path toward censorship. And it is a terrible path. Where does one draw the line? The issue was made clear—amusingly or frighteningly so, depending on your viewpoint—in an op-ed page article in *The New York Times* by Matthew L. Miller, then a recent graduate of the Columbia Law School. "You won't find a proposal to edit Humphrey Bogart's films on Congress's agenda right now," he wrote. "But if pending legislation to ban all cigarette advertisements is enacted, you may want to Betamax 'Casablanca' before the government gets to it. . . . Bogie's suave way of lighting up on the late show surely does as much to glamorize cigarettes as the Marlboro Man. If one has to go, doesn't the other? . . . If the desire to change our minds about smoking is allowed to justify a ban on advertising, what is there in principle to prevent the government from interfering with every communication that makes smoking look like fun? Movies in which happy lovers share a smoke could be edited; heroines who puff in novels could be excised; Noel Coward's plays might become downright illegal to stage. No doubt the proponents of a ban would stop short of tampering with every work of stage, screen, and literature. The logic of their proposal, however, is not so restrained. . . . To say that we shouldn't be free to hear about what we're still free to do is the first step towards banning Bogie."

Or newsclips of Franklin Roosevelt. Or pictures of Kentucky's Senator Wendell Ford. Or the millions of others, famous and infamous and unfamous, who smoke.

But government-financed antismoking ads would not lead to banning Bogie and would not lead to censorship. Instead, they would provide the "more speech rather than less" that Sack and others who cherish the Bill of Rights prefer.

Certainly, it is the role of the government to deal with social issues. And certainly the government, be it conservative or liberal, fulfills this role. In June 1988, the government spent $17 million sending every household in the nation a pamphlet with straight talk about AIDS, about how you get it and how you don't. It spends more than $1 billion a year on medical programs for veterans, and more than $7 billion a year on medical research. States spend millions annually advertising lotteries whose social usefulness is questionable. Certainly, federal allocations for advertisements that have a proven ability to persuade people to quit smoking could be justified socially, economically, and constitutionally.

Chapter 5
Will Truth Out?

In these health-conscious days, it has become fashionable for commentators on all sides to join the ban-the-cigarette-ad campaign, usually out of sincere belief that smoking is deadly. It is, of course, but so is tampering with freedom. Liberals back the ban in the interests of social reform. Conservatives back it in the guise of paternalistic concern for the weak of will. And the weakest, these commentators argue, are our children.

Consider the position of George Will, the conservative columnist, television commentator, friend of first ladies, and Chicago Cubs fan: "Examine the average cigarette advertisement—toothsome young people frolicking in surf, a picture of a mountain meadow, slogans such as 'Get a taste of it' or 'Come to where the flavor is.' Try to measure the information content. Cigarette advertisements are not seminars; they are inducements. . . ." These inducements, he says, are especially effective on young people. "The evidence from the nations with the severest limits on cigarette advertising is that after such advertising is limited, adult smokers continue but fewer young people start." Therefore, says Will, the government should protect the young by limiting what they hear.

As for the First Amendment, Will dismisses it as "an amendment to a political document. Its primary protection is for speech related to the process by which we govern ourselves—the working of representative government and the cultural activities that nourish a free society."

Shouldn't we go further, then, and protect the young from hearing about things other than the social joys of smoking? Shouldn't we protect them from hearing about the pleasures of sex? Why not ban advertising for explicit books and movies and even suggestive clothes? Liquor kills, just as cigarettes do. Sex, through AIDS, kills. And what about the sun? Should we allow Florida to advertise the joys of sunshine now that we know that the sun causes cancer?

Will is not far from banning Bogie. But tobacco is unique, argue those who favor banning cigarette ads. The Toronto *Globe and Mail*, announcing in 1986 that it would no longer run tobacco ads, offered this explanation: "Why single out tobacco? Because unlike even alcohol, whose abuse can destroy the lives of drinkers and create other victims, tobacco is unsafe when used *precisely the way the manufacturer intends* [emphasis in original]." Ban proponents always argue that a tobacco ad ban would not lead down the slippery slope to prohibiting other forms of advertising as well. "Tobacco is a unique danger," asserts a 1986 New York State Bar Association report by lawyer Henry C. Miller. "To say we cannot distinguish between tobacco and other products is absurd. It's the difference between the bubonic plague and the common cold."

The slippery slope argument, ban proponents say, wrongly assumes that legislators and judges do not know how to draw distinctions. As evidence, they note that the broadcast ban on tobacco ads has been in effect for more than fifteen years without spreading to other products.

In fact, every time commercial speech is singled out for censorship—gambling ads, ads for lawyers or doctors—advocates always argue that the speech is somehow "unique" and that the regulation would not be extended.

Will and others focus on the effect of cigarette advertising on minors. Some witnesses at congressional hearings have contended that cigarette advertising actually is targeted at minors; since cigarette sales to minors are illegal in all but six states, they argue, all cigarette advertising itself should be illegal. After 1987 hearings on the ad-ban proposals, Wally Snyder, a senior vice president of the American Advertising Federation, said the emphasis on minors represented a new way to justify a ban on otherwise-protected speech. It is a backdoor approach to fiddling with freedom of expression.

"Rep. Synar acknowledged that establishing a link between tobacco ads and minors might help overcome the First Amendment problems that hinder other congressmen from jumping onto the ad-ban wagon," *Advertising Age*, the trade publication, reported.

But this line of reasoning seems weak. Thirty years ago, the Supreme Court ruled that it was wrong to "reduce the adult population . . . to reading only what is fit for children." Hollywood can make movies that cater to adults. Publishers can print books that are suitable mainly for adults. Editors can edit magazines with adult audiences in mind. It stands to reason that manufacturers can make products intended for use by adults and advertise those products, even if impressionable youngsters might see—and be enticed by—those advertisements.

Guy L. Smith IV, publisher of *Philip Morris* magazine, put a somewhat finer edge on this same point in 1987 in a guest column in *Adweek*. "There is simply no way to make an ad disappear should a child view it—no way other than censorship. But . . . limiting all information to that which is palatable to a child is unacceptable. The same logic would strip the libraries of great literature, the museums of great art and the media of any information that is remotely reflective of reality in today's troubled world."

Apart from all this, there is evidence that advertising is not a significant influence on the decision by young people to smoke. On the contrary, say some experts, advertising is one of the least significant factors influencing smoking by teenagers. Dr. Scott Ward, author and professor of marketing at the University of Pennsylvania's Wharton School, maintains that those who favor banning tobacco advertising wrongly assert that such advertising causes children and teenagers to decide to smoke. Ward testified at a House subcommittee hearing last year that "the available evidence indicates that advertising is among the least influential factors involved—certainly not influential enough to warrant an advertising ban, even if we agreed that it is proper for the government to try to manipulate consumer behavior by suppressing information."

Ward testified that the most forceful determinants of smoking are parents and peers, both of whom "are much more important determinants of children's developing consumer behavior patterns than advertising." He concluded: "Most teenagers choose not to smoke, responding to the positive and negative influences in a manner that should satisfy antitobacco advocates. My own study of over 600 children and their parents demonstrated that even young children can and do develop skills to evaluate advertising."

So the idea of shielding children from advertising in order to protect them from the evils of smoking seems ill-advised.

It has no ground in the law.

It has no ground in marketing.

It has no ground in psychology.

The best way to convince your children not to smoke is simply to quit smoking yourself.

The worst way to teach them about democracy is to allow their freedoms to be chipped away.

The Evidence on Advertising

The purpose of those who would ban advertising of cigarettes is to reduce, or even eliminate, cigarette use in the United States. The American Medical Association's publicly proclaimed goal is to create a smoke-free society by the year 2000. It's unlikely, though, that a ban would significantly reduce cigarette use. Numerous independent studies of tobacco advertising in the United States have concluded that there is no significant correlation between the overall volume of tobacco advertising and aggregate consumer demand. According to these studies, advertising mostly reallocates market shares among the different brands of cigarettes.

Sixteen nations have had bans in effect for ten years or more, providing a vast amount of data on the effect that bans have on overall cigarette usage. In most of these countries, tobacco consumption has actually *increased*. Here, from a 1986 study by the International Advertising Association (IAA), is the growth in per capita cigarette consumption in eight Communist-bloc countries between 1970 and 1984—years in which all tobacco advertising was banned:

USSR: Up 10 percent
Poland: Up 14 percent
Hungary: Up 23 percent
Romania: Up 23 percent
Czechoslovakia: Up 32 percent
Bulgaria: Up 36 percent
Yugoslavia: Up 47 percent
East Germany: Up 54 percent

In all, per capita cigarette consumption in these Communist-bloc nations grew an average of 16 percent a year. Overall cigarette consumption increased by 30 percent.

A table of the annual compounded growth rate in per capita cigarette consumption, through 1984, for seven non-Communist countries in which advertising was banned appears at the top of page 39.

Italy, Iceland, Singapore, Finland, Thailand, and Taiwan all have partial or complete tobacco ad bans, and in each of them the consumption of cigarettes has increased. Further, in Norway, where per capita consumption was declining before a ban was enacted in 1975, the trend reversed itself in 1981; since then, per capita consumption has actually increased.

Nation	Year of Ban	Growth Rate (percent)
Norway	1975	- 0.5
Iceland	1972	0.8
Singapore	1970	0.9
Finland	1978	1.8
Thailand	1969	3.0
Italy	1962	3.2
Taiwan	1970	4.3

In the Soviet Union and China, where there is no cigarette advertising, consumption is also on the rise.

The IAA world study concluded: "There is no evidence from those countries where tobacco advertising has been banned, that the ban has been accompanied by any significant reduction in overall consumption, per-capita consumption or the incidence of smoking. *The market trends apparent prior to the introduction of a ban have largely continued unchanged in the years following it.* On the other hand, there is some evidence that the absence of advertising can significantly hold back the development of new and more advanced tobacco products." The study went on to note that "in Sweden, where tobacco advertising is permitted, albeit on a restricted basis, the penetration of lower-tar cigarettes is significantly higher than in Norway and Finland, where tobacco advertising is banned."

A similar situation occurred in the United States. In the 1950s, tobacco companies, seeking to meet consumer tastes, reduced the amount of tar and nicotine in their cigarettes by 30 to 40 percent. Then, in 1960, the Federal Trade Commission helped bring about an industrywide ban on the advertising of tar and nicotine content. Some twenty-five years later FTC chairman Daniel Oliver stated in a letter to a congressman studying the impact of banning cigarette ads, "Because the consumer no longer received information on tar and nicotine content, it was no longer advantageous for cigarette firms to compete to reduce those substances, and they stopped. . . . Subsequently, many public-service organizations decried the ban, the FTC changed its policy, firms began again to compete with regard to tar and nicotine content—and began again to advertise tar and nicotine content—and tar and nicotine levels once again went down." Then, when television advertising of cigarettes was banned, tar and nicotine levels rose once more.

Not everyone agrees that overseas bans have been a failure. Former Federal Trade Commission chairman Michael Pertschuk, writing in *The Nation* last year, compared third world countries "where cigarette companies dominate the media [and] the amount of cigarette smoking is rapidly increasing" with countries such as Canada, the United States, and Britain, where bans on broadcast advertising have been accompanied by substantial reductions in the percentage of smokers in their populations. Surgeon General C. Everett Koop, in an appearance on "Face the Nation" in 1985, said, "If I had my way, I would certainly ban advertising. The experience in countries where advertising bans have been enforced has shown a tremendous drop in smoking."

Detractors point to several flaws in the IAA and similar studies of tobacco advertising overseas. For one thing, they point out that tobacco advertising is only one factor influencing the decision to smoke; others include social, religious, and familial smoking behavior and attitudes, price and disposable income, age, intelligence, and social class. It is impossible to determine the effect of one factor, such as advertising, without holding the others constant, and of course those other factors are constantly changing, the critics contend.

Some observers also question whether studies from other countries and other cultures can be used to predict behavior in the United States. The IAA study, for instance, does not take into account differences in social circumstances and government regulation. For example, the IAA study cites the Soviet Union as an example of a country that has no advertising but heavy tobacco consumption. However, tobacco is extremely inexpensive in the Soviet Union, and there are virtually no smoking-control measures.

Ban proponents also question the assertion that advertising affects only brand loyalty. In any given year, they say, only 10 percent of all smokers switch brands. Moreover, the 250 brands currently on the market are made by only six companies. Surely, they say, those companies would not spend $2.5 billion a year simply to get smokers to switch. How much money to spend, and how to spend it, of course, are decisions for business, not outsiders.

The experts thus are split on the likely effects of an advertising ban. But even if the experts could agree that a ban would reduce domestic consumption, it would still be a bad idea. It is not the government's responsibility to reduce cigarette consumption. It is the government's responsibility to assure that people have all the information they need to make an informed personal decision about smoking.

Government should not be permitted to impose ignorance as a means of changing people's behavior. As John Seigenthaler, president of the American Society of Newspaper Editors and editor of the *Nashville Tennessean*, told the House subcommittee considering the Synar bill in 1987, "We always have protected our citizens from allegedly offensive or harmful information by providing more, not less information. Our Founding Fathers were clear and correct in their belief that the antidote for allegedly harmful speech is not government-imposed censorship, but more speech from more sources, calculated to permit the individual to make free, informed choices."

There is no question that smoking poses the greatest threat to our national health. Consider the evidence:

- The surgeon general has identified cigarette smoking as irrefutably the single most preventable cause of death in America.
- More than 350,000 Americans die from cigarette smoking each year.
- The percentage of women smokers between ages twenty and twenty-four actually increased from 1980 to 1985.
- Exposure to tobacco smoke increases the incidence of lung cancer in nonsmokers.
- Smoking is responsible for one-quarter of all deaths caused by fire.
- Smoking during pregnancy increases the risk of premature birth, spontaneous abortion, and stillbirth.
- The federal government spends more than $4 billion annually to treat smoking-related illnesses.

But should America do anything to curb tobacco advertising in the face of this devastation? No.

The premise of the First Amendment is that if the antismoking interests and the tobacco industry are left to compete in the marketplace of ideas, the truth about smoking will prevail. The experience of the antismoking ads in the 1960s bears this out. The right answer is to use all available information to persuade people not to smoke. The wrong answer is to stifle speech about smoking.

Chapter 6
Fairness in Advertising

To date, cigarettes have been the chief target of those who would seek to alter our behavior by limiting our freedoms. But alcohol advertising is surely the next frontier. Already, numerous restrictions have been imposed in this area. Three federal agencies now regulate the advertising of alcohol. The Bureau of Alcohol, Tobacco and Firearms, a branch of the Treasury Department, controls advertising under the Federal Alcohol Administration Act of 1935. This act bars, among other things, advertisements that contain false, misleading, obscene, or indecent statements in alcohol ads, though it's unclear what an obscene statement, let alone an indecent one, might be. The bureau also has established rules requiring that ads disclose a liquor's alcohol content.

The Federal Trade Commission can regulate advertising for alcohol if it determines the advertising to be unfair or deceptive under the Federal Trade Commission Act. Unfair advertising is that which causes unavoidable harm to consumers, through, for example, misleading representations. Deceptive advertising is defined as that which can deceive a large number of the persons reading or viewing the ad.

Finally, the Federal Communications Commission can become involved if it determines that broadcast advertising of liquor and beer presents a one-sided view of an important public controversy. In such a case, the commission could in theory allow groups like Project SMART (Stop Marketing Alcohol on Radio and Television) to air counteradvertising. (This would be done under the Fairness Doctrine, which the FCC has abandoned but which Congress is intent on reinstating.)

Below the federal level, six states now limit or ban some forms of advertising of alcoholic beverages, and many more are considering such legislation. The restrictions range from an outright ban of most forms of intrastate liquor advertising, in Mississippi and Utah, to a prohibition of off-premises advertising of beer prices, in Ohio. A federal appeals court has upheld the Mississippi statute, and the Supreme Court of the United States refused to review that ruling.

The states derive their power to control advertising from the Twenty-first Amendment, which ended Prohibition. It states, in part: "The transportation or importation into any State, Territory, or possession of the United States for delivery or use therein of intoxicating liquors, *in violation of the laws thereof*, is hereby prohibited." State courts have generally interpreted this to mean that, in the area of alcohol, states' rights supersede citizens'—and advertisers'—rights under the First Amendment.

The Supreme Court has never dealt with this issue directly, but, judging from its ruling in *Posadas*, the Court might uphold a ban on liquor advertising even if it determined that the Twenty-first Amendment did not override the First.

But would that be in the interest of the people? Not at all. An alcohol advertising ban presents many of the same problems as a tobacco advertising ban:

- It would erode product improvement incentives.
- It would be ineffective in promoting public-health objectives, since there is no clear evidence that alcohol advertising increases overall alcohol consumption.
- It could lead to the censorship of other products.

But, as with tobacco, the principal objection to an alcohol ad ban is that it would be inconsistent with democracy and First Amendment values. As three advertising trade groups wrote in a joint 1986 statement, a ban on all alcohol advertising would be an attempt "to have government impose itself as national censor to protect consumers from themselves through the suppression of information. Such an approach is totally inconsistent with a free society."

So whether it's advertising cigarettes that cause cancer, or liquor that leads to 25,000 automobile deaths every year, or condoms that lead to the premature sex education of youngsters, or lottery tickets that entice the poor to spend their food money on one-in-a-million chances for riches, the principle remains the same:

Truthful advertising of lawful products is part of the American economic system. Truthful advertising of lawful products is part of the American system of democracy. As New York University law professor Burt Neuborne said recently before the House Committee on Energy and Commerce:

> The free flow of speech about commercial options deserves special protection because it is critical to our culture's commitment to freedom of choice and individual autonomy. Attempts to limit the flow of truthful information about lawful choices—whether economic or political—are simply disguised means of government manipulation of individual behavior through the use of information rationing. Nothing could be more inconsistent with—and more corrosive of—a commitment to individual dignity and free choice than a regime of commercial censorship that purports to assure consumers the freedom to choose, while secretly stacking the information deck to manipulate their choices. . . . The result is the illusion of freedom; but the reality of government control.

Bans constitute "regulation by stealth." Governments purport to leave people free to choose, but then use bans to deprive them of all the information necessary to make a well-informed choice. Any ban of truthful speech about a lawful product violates our deep commitment to the notion that people can be trusted to make wise decisions if they only have access to all relevant information.

Chapter 7
Paternalism vs. Democracy

If there is any instance "where a state can escape First Amendment constraint while prohibiting truthful advertising promoting lawful sales," it is in the regulation of liquor advertising, a federal court of appeals noted in upholding Mississippi's restrictions on liquor advertising. For, under our Constitution, the Twenty-first Amendment represents the only express grant of specific power to the states.

Yet states routinely restrict the rights of advertisers to speak freely and truthfully. In 1981, the supreme court of Nevada upheld the constitutionality of a state law that prohibited brothels from advertising in counties where prostitution was illegal—even though the brothels themselves were situated in counties that allowed prostitution. There is a "common-sense distinction between speech proposing a commercial transaction, which occurs in an area traditionally subject to government regulation, and other varieties of speech," the Nevada court declared in *Princess Sea Industries v. State.* Thus, it said, commercial speech has "a limited measure of protection commensurate with its subordinate position in the scale of First Amendment values, [and] modes of regulation that might be impermissible in the realm of noncommercial expression" are allowed. A concurring opinion noted that "the state does not lose its power to regulate commercial activity deemed harmful to the public whenever speech is a component of that activity."

It wasn't explained how speech about prostitution is harmful to the public when prostitution itself is apparently deemed harmless—at least in certain counties.

Several states regulate truthful advertising by medical doctors. In addition to banning false, fraudulent, misleading, or deceptive ads, the Board of Medical Examiners of the state of New Jersey prohibits advertising that lists claims of superiority, that offers free or discounted services, or that contains testimonials from satisfied patients. The board also requires that ads from doctors be "presented in a dignified manner without the use of drawing, animations, dramatizations, music, lyrics, or clinical photographs."

In California, the state supreme court has upheld regulations requiring that qualifying statements in ads for automobiles be large enough and displayed long enough for an average reader or viewer to understand. "Such regulations can be broader than statutes regulating other speech because the danger of a chilling effect on protected speech is not present," the court ruled in the 1982 case of *Ford Dealers Association v. Department of Motor Vehicles.*

These rules and regulations usually are based on a state's desire to protect the health, welfare, or safety of its residents. To many legislators and bureaucrats, that desire takes precedence over the citizens' rights to speak or write freely. Thus, while it's perfectly legal in North Dakota to own a pistol, the North Dakota code prohibits pistol dealers from placing placards in their windows announcing the fact that pistols are for sale inside.

"Legislative regulation of products or activities deemed harmful, such as cigarettes, alcoholic beverages, and prostitution, has varied from outright prohibition on the one hand . . . to legalization of the product or activity with restrictions on stimulation of its demand on the other hand," the Supreme Court wrote in *Posadas,* in which it upheld the ban on advertising of casino gambling in Puerto Rico, even though the gambling itself was legal. "To rule out the latter, intermediate kind of response would require more than we find in the First Amendment."

When it comes to the free-speech rights of advertisers, no group is more aggrieved, perhaps, than the nation's lawyers, a quarter of whom now advertise. Though a series of Supreme Court rulings has lifted some of the stricter restrictions on advertising by lawyers, at last count twenty-five states had rules or laws requiring that such advertising be "dignified." Iowa is typical. Initially, ads there were restricted to displays of words and numbers accompanied by a single "nondramatic" voice. Now the state allows pictures in lawyers' television commercials but bars the use of background music and so-called live action. "Electronic media advertising, when contrasted with printed advertising, tolerates much less deliberation by those at whom it is aimed," the Iowa supreme court has stated, adding that it thus has a "very real potential for abuse." The U.S. Supreme Court has refused to consider the constitutionality of these rules. It has also let stand a California rule that bars lawyers from using testimonials or client endorsements in ads.

The Supreme Court did rule on one aspect of lawyer advertising in mid-1988. In a six-to-three ruling (Reagan appointees O'Connor and Scalia joined Chief Justice Rehnquist in the dissent), the Court ruled that states may not bar lawyers from using truthful direct-mail solicitation in an effort to woo clients. The case arose in 1985 when the Kentucky supreme court refused to allow Louisville lawyer Richard Shapero to send letters to homeowners facing foreclosure. The U.S. Supreme Court ruled that states could make lawyers submit their letters for screening to weed out the "truthful from the false, the helpful from the misleading, and the harmless from the harmful." And it did not tamper with state-imposed restrictions on in-person solicitation of clients by lawyers. Still, those lawyers who favor advertising considered the ruling a major victory for their profession.

Justice William Brennan, who wrote the opinion, drew a distinction between letters and in-person solicitation: "A truthful and non-deceptive letter, no matter how big its type . . . can never shout at the recipient or grasp him by the lapels, as can a lawyer engaging in face-to-face solicitation. Unlike the potential client who has a badgering advocate breathing down his neck, the recipient of a letter . . . can effectively avoid further bombardment by averting his eyes." Brennan added: "Merely because targeted, direct-mail solicitation presents lawyers with opportunities for isolated abuses or mistakes does not justify a total ban on that mode of protected commercial speech."

Those seeking to ban or censor truthful advertising—be it for a product or a service—have in common paternalism and arrogance. Both were evident in the comment of a spokesman for the Kentucky Bar Association (KBA), which opposed lawyer Shapero's solicitation letter. If Shapero were "but a tradesman seeking to hawk his wares," he would have been entitled to win, the KBA said. Lawyers, it implied, are special.

Those who would regulate advertising of doctors say doctors are special, of course, and those who would censor the advertising of automobile dealers say automobile dealers are special. The consumer must be protected—even from truthful information—say these paternalistic censors. That flies in the face of democracy. As Justice Brandeis noted in 1927:

To [the Framers], courageous, self-reliant men, with confidence in the power of free and fearless reasoning applied through the processes of popular government, no danger flowing from speech can be deemed clear and present, unless the incidence of the evil apprehended is so imminent that it may befall before there is opportunity for full discussion. If there be time to expose through discussion the falsehood and fallacies, to avert the evil by the processes of education, the remedy to be applied is more speech, not enforced silence.

The States Exempt Themselves

Not surprisingly, when it comes to advertising their own businesses, states pull out all the stops. They don't ban or censor advertisements that help fill their own coffers—even if the product advertised is thought by some to be the devil's own doing.

Consider the advertising of lotteries. In the late 1800s, the federal government passed some laws that were designed primarily to prevent the spread of privately owned, unregulated lotteries, many of which were "generally fraudulent wagering schemes." Over the years, the laws have been amended and rewritten. Today, it is against the law to:

- Use the mails for conducting or promoting a lottery, except for state-operated lotteries that are sending information to state residents or residents of adjoining states.
- Mail any newspaper, circular, pamphlet, or publication of any kind that contains any advertisement for a lottery, or that contains any list of the prizes drawn or awarded by means of such lottery. State-operated lotteries in the home state and adjacent states are not subject to this restriction.
- Broadcast any advertisements or news about lotteries other than state-sanctioned games.

Lotteries were thought to be evil until 1964. That's when the New Hampshire legislature established a sweepstakes to help finance local education. Since then, half the states and the District of Columbia have established their own lotteries, and there's at least one joint lottery run by half-a-dozen states. The states now see the games in a new light: not as evil schemes that drain food money from the poor and offer astronomical odds, but as revenue-building enterprises that finance roads, schools, parks, and services for old people. Lotteries, say state servants, are the equivalent of a voluntary tax.

Naturally, the state officials who run lotteries want to sell as many tickets as possible. So they advertise. (First, of course, they had to get

Congress to pass exceptions to the postal laws; that was accomplished in 1975 without much effort.) In Iowa alone—a state that won't let lawyers play music in their ads—the state lottery spends $6 million a year on promotion (including a catchy jingle). Overall, states spend about $188 million annually to promote their lotteries, according to *Gaming and Wagering Business* magazine. That's 1.3 percent of sales. Not surprisingly, the state paternalism that seeks to protect citizens from advertisements for legal brothels, legal liquor, and legal services by doctors and lawyers vanishes when it comes to ads for state-sanctioned lotteries.

Of course, ads for nonstate lotteries—buy a ticket and win a new Ford at the local supermarket—remain out of bounds.

All of this runs counter to the argument that legislators and judges most frequently cite in support of restrictions on truthful commercial speech—that the public is somehow vulnerable or unsophisticated and thus needs protection from the truthful statements of manufacturers of legal products and purveyors of lawful services. For if the purveyor is the state, all bets are off.

(The Reagan administration, clearly of two minds on matters of commercial speech, has supported a bill that would permit *nationwide* advertising of state-authorized lotteries. Douglas M. Kmiec, a deputy assistant attorney general, testified before Congress in 1987 that restrictions on the advertising of lotteries are "inconsistent with the notion, which is fundamental to both our government and our economy, that people can be trusted to make wise decisions if they have access to all relevant information." That, of course, is not the view of Reagan appointees to the Supreme Court.)

Compare what's permitted in advertising for lotteries to that permitted for securities, in which a purchaser's chances of success are much greater. There are no jingle-filled television ads urging you to buy stock in General Electric. There are no billboards urging you to play the Wall Street game. There are no newspaper advertisements outlining the good things to come for investors in General Motors.

Why not? Subparagraph (b)(1) of Section 5 of the Securities Act of 1933 prohibits the use of interstate commerce or the mails—including any writing or television or radio material—to offer stock or security for sale. In other words, you can't set up a company and take out an ad in the local paper telling of the wonders of that company and asking readers to buy its stock, even if every word is fair and accurate and truthful and bland. All you can do is take out a so-called tombstone ad that states where a prospectus can be obtained. The aim, of course, is to "protect" the investors, who might otherwise throw away their money on get-rich-quick schemes with enormous odds against a payoff—schemes like, say, a lottery.

"Prior to the [1933] act, slick operators were selling stock in gold mines that never existed, in companies with absolutely no assets, in lakefront land with no lakes," says Jeffrey Bartell, a former securities commissioner for the state of Wisconsin. "The Securities Act of 1933 was one of the best consumer-protection laws ever passed by Congress." His view is widely held.

One man's consumer protection is another's censorship, of course. And there are those who believe that the Securities and Exchange Commission's regulation of new securities issues constitutes an unconstitutional prior restraint on protected commercial speech. According to a 1984 article in the *St. John's Law Review*, "Statutory provisions that grant the Commission power to review documents before they become . . . public, strengthened by the availability of criminal sanctions and SEC injunctions, essentially authorize the SEC to exercise the functions of a censor, and thus present serious issues of prior restraint and 'chilling.'" The article concluded that "SEC restriction of speech is pervasive, and no longer can be ignored."

In a free-market economy, "the free flow of commercial information is indispensable," the Supreme Court declared twelve years ago in *Virginia Pharmacy*. But the strict rules on securities advertising remain in effect. As in nearly every instance of restrictions on truthful commercial speech, the consumer is thus *deprived* of information that might help him make an intelligent decision affecting his life and livelihood. Controls on the form and content of advertising—controls such as Tom Goldstein has proposed for cigarette advertising or controls like the tombstone ads mandated for the securities industry—are just as pernicious as outright bans.

Content-based restrictions are particularly pernicious when they deprive the commercial message of its ability to get the consumers' attention. Advertisers know that the most effective way to get a message across is to mix information with "noncognitive" forms of persuasion, such as music and color. But regulators can make ads so dull and gray that no one pays any attention to them.

New York University law professor Burt Neuborne testified in Congress about this problem in April 1987: "The distinction between falsity and effectiveness must be strictly respected. Censorship that drains a commercial message of the capacity to command attention and persuade effectively is not a legitimate exercise in preventing false advertising, but an indirect attempt to censor the speech by reducing it to an anodyne bromide."

It is possible, in other words, to censor by making something so unattractive and unappealing that no one will pay attention to it. Look at a tombstone ad. Then listen to the jingle urging you to buy a ticket—to "play"—in the Iowa state lottery. Is there not an imbalance here? Could it be because, in one instance, the state is the regulator, and, in the other, it's the businessman?

Is that the way it's supposed to be in a democracy?

The Worst Offenders

Advertisers face censorship from other than legislators and the courts, of course. Newspapers and broadcasters themselves are probably the strictest censors of advertising in this country.

"I don't think anybody in his right mind believes that a great newspaper's purpose is just to make money or that its greatness is defined by how much money it makes," Leonard Silk, economics columnist for *The New York Times*, said in 1982 at a conference on "The Responsibilities of Journalists." Four years later, journalist Tom Goldstein, commenting on Silk's statement in a Twentieth Century Fund Paper, asserted that "these days, newspapers seem preoccupied with profits." Otherwise, he posited, they would adjust their cigarette advertising policies to match the antismoking position enunciated on their editorial pages. The consistent and pure publisher, he said, would ban cigarette advertising if on his editorial pages he opposed smoking.

But that's wrong. Carried to its logical conclusion, such an approach would require the consistent and pure publisher to leave out all *news* of cigarettes or tobacco in his newspaper as well. And if he opposed "Star Wars," he would not allow any *news* of Star Wars. In fact, the consistent and pure publisher of a general-interest publication takes advertisements for any product or service that is legal, subject to the same standards that the publisher uses to decide what goes into the news columns: the material must be accurate, and it must be tasteful.

But not all publishers and broadcasters are consistent and pure. "Most American newspapers routinely publish editorials condemning censorship in any form," David Shaw, a reporter for the *Los Angeles Times*, wrote in 1987. "But they regularly impose specific restrictions on the size, content, language, and illustrations of advertising in their pages, especially advertising for X-rated movies and other violent and sexually oriented films."

Of course, restrictions are imposed on the content, language, and illustrations used in *news* stories, too, especially news stories relating to sex and sexually explicit crimes and violence. Still, the advertising policies generally are much more censorial than the news policies. The *Cleveland Plain Dealer*, for instance, has long imposed a ban on ads for handguns, escort services, and fortune tellers. There's no similar news ban. Overall, Shaw estimates that more than 300 of the nation's 1,700 daily newspapers currently have formal prohibitions on advertising for various products and services.

It's worse with television. According to an article in *The Wall Street Journal* (which itself shuns gun advertisements), TV censors won't allow ads showing people taking pills, even antacids or aspirin.

They won't allow ads showing toilet paper hanging next to a toilet.

They won't show advertising for hard liquor.

They won't show a tampon in a tampon ad or let douche makers explain just what a douche is used for.

They won't show an ad in which someone burps.

They won't show an armpit in a deodorant ad.

They won't show people drinking in a beer ad.

Of course, any publisher or station owner has the right to determine what ads to run and what ads not to run. Freedom to censor—news or ads—is certainly the legitimate flip side of freedom to print. But it's wrong. Refusing to run an ad, except for reasons of accuracy or taste, is censorship.

Sometimes the networks' censorial tendencies extend to so-called issue ads as well. In 1986, for instance, all three networks refused an ad from W. R. Grace & Co. on the federal deficit until Grace agreed to change the wording.

"Democracy depends on citizens' having access to a free marketplace of ideas," Stephen Elliott, the director of corporate advertising for Grace, wrote at the time the ads were barred. "We recognize and respect the First Amendment rights of the networks, and all we hoped was that they would respect our First Amendment rights to speak out."

This aspect of commercial speech gets little attention because it's *private*, as opposed to public, censorship. But private censorship is dangerous as well, for three reasons: One is that it could lead to increasing calls for legislation to guarantee access to the media, legislation that is fraught with peril. The second is that, as Elliott noted, such censorship restricts the free marketplace of ideas. The third is that those who would advocate public censorship can use the fact of private censorship to bolster their arguments.

"It's a free country," Eugene Patterson, the chairman of the *St. Petersburg Times*, has written, but:

> a newspaper that chooses not to print news or lawful advertising simply because it editorially disagrees with the thrust of the information is, in my judgment, blinding a community to what is going on in its midst. A community so blinded has no basis for deciding whether it approves or disapproves. The newspaper has presumed not simply to recommend standards editorially; it has decided it will enforce its predilections on others by censoring reality.

Erwin Kroll, the editor of *The Progressive*, a feisty magazine that defends the rights of the unpopular, once wrote a memorandum to his publisher putting forth arguments similar to Patterson's:

> We abhor censorship in all its many forms. We've paid a heavy price, at times, for taking that position—e.g., for defending the free-speech rights of Nazis and Klansmen—but I believe we can take much pride in never having compromised the principle.
> The magazine's advertising policy should be considered in that context—that is, our commitment to promoting the broadest possible freedom of expression. . . . I am convinced that we should *never* reject an ad because we disagree with or disapprove of the individual or organization sponsoring the ad, or because we have political objections to the content. There is no reason at all to shield *The Progressive's* readers from ideas—or, for that matter, from products—that we find troublesome, unappealing, unfortunate, or just plain wrong. . . .

Goldstein and others disagree. "Publishers need not synchronize their advertising and editorial policies," he concludes. "But there are special circumstances—like advertisements for patent medicines at the turn of the century, like advertisements for abortion clinics in Chicago, and like advertisements for cigarets—where publishers can apply to their advertising columns some of the same zeal they reserve for their editorial pages, thereby enhancing their credibility and proving they are socially responsible."

Maybe that would enhance credibility, and maybe it would represent some sort of social responsibility. But it would deprive the reader or the viewer of a different perspective, of another source of information.

That's censorship, and it is dreadful whether set in motion by a paternalistic government or a socially responsible, credible publisher.

Chapter 8
Conclusion

Censorship is contagious.

"Censorship is habit-forming," Floyd Abrams, a lawyer who specializes in First Amendment cases, told a meeting of the American Bar Association. "We have always lived in a country that understood that, even as to speech of which we disapproved, even as to speech which we feared, even as to commercial speech which we disdained or had concern about. It is at the heart of the First Amendment that we do not lightly strike out at speech to deal with social problems. . . . Censorship, ladies and gentlemen, once established takes on a life of its own. That is the lesson of history."

That certainly is the lesson of history as far as commercial speech is concerned. In the early decades of this democracy, there was no censorship of commercial messages. According to the best evidence we have, there was no distinction between speech concerning the marketplace of ideas and that concerning the ideas of the marketplace. Speech was free, as mandated by the men who wrote and enacted the Bill of Rights. "Here we are not afraid to follow truth whether it may lead, nor to tolerate any error so long as reason is left free to combat it," Thomas Jefferson wrote in a letter to an English historian in 1820.

Today this notion of an informed citizenry, capable of making rational decisions, has been replaced by paternalistic arguments based on the benefits of public ignorance. Such paternalism leads, ultimately, to totalitarianism. It is this big stew of ideas and information that distinguishes a democracy from other forms of government. The more censorship there is—be it public censorship by well-meaning judges and legislators or private censorship by misguided and misinformed members of the media—the less democracy there is.

And nowhere is there more censorship in this nation than in the area of commercial speech. It serves no purpose. It serves up great harm. In summary, here's how censorship in this area works:

1. Cigarette ads are barred from television and radio.

The purpose: presumably, to protect the public health. Congress has barred cigarette ads from television and radio; yet an estimated 350,000 Americans die each year from cigarette smoking, and smoking-related diseases cost the U.S. health-care system an estimated $22 billion a year, of which some $4.2 billion comes from the federal government. In light of the magnitude of the problem, it is quite likely that Congress will institute a wider advertising ban.

The harm: There will be a decline in the introduction of new, less harmful products. There will be a decline in the competition among brands. There will be a decline in price competition. There will be a lessening of debate over cigarettes and health. According to many experts, there will be no accompanying decline in cigarette consumption. There will be no reduction in lung cancer. There will still be one million new smokers in this country every year, including boys and girls who will continue to take up smoking as long as cigarettes remain legal.

But even if ad bans worked, they would be destructive. For they would drive a wedge in our democracy. "By selectively deciding what commercial messages may be heard by the populace, the censor acquires enormous power over the behavior patterns of an entire society," Professor Neuborne testified. "Whether the censor elects to use this enormous power to manipulate individual behavior on the basis of health or morals or efficiency or mere whim, the shift of power from the individual to the State is stunning."

2.   Liquor ads are controlled by several states.

The purpose: to control drinking and the damage that flows from it.

The harm: The free-enterprise system becomes less free, even as alcohol abuse continues unabated. A government-sanctioned, even government-abetted, price-fixing scheme sets in. Drunks continue to drive and to kill themselves and others. The problem of alcoholism and its trauma doesn't diminish.

3. Lottery ads and information are barred, in various degrees, from appearing in newspapers and being broadcast over the air.

The purpose: social engineering.

The harm: Lotteries continue, in legal and illegal forms. The states themselves see the revenue possibilities in lotteries, so they set up their own enterprises and carve out an exception to the advertising ban. The original ban then is exposed as a sham, an attempt to modify behavior in a way that circumvents the democratic process.

The list goes on and on. Lawyers can't approach potential clients to solicit business, but aluminum-siding salesmen can. Doctors can't offer testimonials, but summer camps can. Cigarette makers can't advertise on buses in Utah, but junk-food purveyors can. Sellers of securities can't give much more than their name, address, and serial number, but magazine-sweepstakes schemes can bombard you with rush-rush-rush messages and glorious tales of million-dollar winners.

"No differences between commercial and other kinds of speech justify protecting commercial speech less extensively where . . . the government seeks to manipulate private behavior by depriving citizens of truthful information concerning lawful activities," Justice Brennan wrote in 1986.

That was in a dissent. The Chief Justice of the United States is of the opinion that commercial speech is a secondary freedom. But if commercial speech is a secondary freedom, then eventually noncommercial speech will become one too. For in a democracy whose cornerstones are free speech and free enterprise, one type of speech cannot safely be separated from the other.

The economic marketplace and the idea marketplace are intertwined. A constraint on one is a constraint on the other. The First Amendment was designed to ensure that this nation's political process functions properly, and free enterprise is basic to the political process. The theory is that if people are informed, they will be able to choose what is best for them and for their nation. Uninformed people make uninformed choices, and uninformed choices often are bad ones. These choices are not limited to the voting booth. Indeed, most of our choices today are *economic* rather than *political*. And, for better or worse, probably more people today are interested in the type of car they buy than the type of councilman they elect, more interested in studying the brands of skis than in studying the position papers of school board candidates.

"In short," Jacob Fuchsberg, a judge on the New York State Court of Appeals, wrote eight years ago, "political freedom may be so dependent on economic freedom that the pursuit of one cannot be readily divorced from the other, certainly not without drastically circumscribing the freedom of people to exercise a choice among basic competing values."

The fact is, commercial speech and noncommercial speech have become so intertwined that they are inseparable.

There is, of course, an alternative approach to the problem, one favored by lawyers and judges and businessmen and professors and others who worry about the rights of Americans as well as their health, welfare, and safety: Fight speech with speech.

Every year, the government spends $180 million to spread its views in 44 languages to 130 million people who listen to the Voice of America. In 1988, the government spent $17 million on a mass mailing that sought to educate every member of every household about AIDS. The government regularly uses speech—in the form of paid advertising—to tell young men and women about the joys of life in the Army, Navy, Air Force, and Marines. The president of the United States regularly uses the media to explain his views to the American people. Every department of government has a vast public relations bureaucracy that sends out a steady stream of words and tapes and films.

All of this is highly effective.

The rate of increase in new cases of AIDS among homosexual men is declining because of an education campaign that publicized the principles of safe sex. Had the government chosen instead to censor, the result would have been very different.

The consumption of cigarettes in America declined when antismoking commercials were aired to counter cigarette commercials. Consumption began rising again when censorship ended debate on the issue.

If the policymakers and people of this nation believe drinking is bad, then they should use legislation to ban the sale of alcohol or persuasion to cut its use. If the policymakers and people of this nation believe that smoking is bad, they should legislate against cigarettes or propagandize against smoking.

But outlawing speech is far more dangerous than outlawing action.

It is also ineffective.

In 1927, Justice Louis Brandeis said that "the fitting remedy for evil counsels is good ones." He added, "believing in the power of reason as applied through public discussion," the men who founded this nation and outlined our liberties "eschewed silence coerced by law—the argument of force in its worst form."

Today, as the attempts to coerce silence mount, the eloquence of Justice Brandeis takes on a new urgency.

For there is no justification for the silence enforced upon us.

It is not justified historically.

It is not justified socially.

It is not justified economically.

Select Bibliography

Abrams, Floyd. "Good Year for the Press, But Not for Advertisers." *National Law Journal* (August 11, 1986), p. S13.

_____. "Restricting Corporate Editorial Comment Hardly Serves the Public." *Los Angeles Daily Journal* (July 9, 1986), p. 4.

"Ads Have First Amendment Rights." *New York Times* (January 9, 1986), sec. A, p. 22.

Alexander, Lawrence. "Commercial Speech and First Amendment Theory." *Northwestern University Law Review* (April 1980), pp. 307-15.

Barnes, Richard L. "A Call for a Value-based Test of Commercial Speech." *Washington University Law Quarterly* (Winter 1985), pp. 649-706.

_____. "Commercial Speech Concerning Unlawful Conduct: Danger." *BYU Law Review* (1984), pp. 457-508.

Barrett, Edward L. "The Uncharted Area: Commercial Speech and the First Amendment." *UCD Law Review* (Spring 1980), pp. 175-209.

"Bates vs. State Bar of Arizona." *Journal of Marketing* (January 1978), pp. 108-9.

Berman, Jeffrey A. "Constitutional Realism: Legislative Bans on Tobacco Advertisements and the First Amendment." *University of Illinois Law Review* (Fall 1986), pp. 1193-1231.

Berman, Jeffrey A. "First Amendment—Commercial Speech—Restrictability." *Illinois Bar Journal* 75 (July 1987), pp. 631-37.

Beschle, Donald L. "Doing Well, Doing Good and Doing Both." *St. Louis University Law Journal* (March 1986), pp. 385-425.

Brannigan, Vincent M. "Can Cigarette Advertising Be Prohibited?" *Journal of Consumer Advertising* (Netherlands) 10 (June 1987), pp. 193-201.

Braun, Stefan. "Should Commercial Speech Be Accorded Prima Facie Constitutional Recognition under the Canadian Charter of Rights and Freedoms?" *Ottawa Law Review* (Winter 1986), pp. 37-53.

Brosnahan, Roger. "Regulation of Lawyer Advertising." *Brooklyn Law Review* (Spring 1980), pp. 423-36.

Brown, Jesse Cecil. "The Impact of Bates." Ph.D. diss., Southern Illinois University at Carbondale, 1982.

Burnett, Barbara A. "Protecting and Regulating Commercial Speech." *Comment* (Summer 1983), pp. 637-80.

Canby, William C. "Commercial Speech of Lawyers." *Brooklyn Law Review* (Spring 1980), pp. 401-22.

Canellos, Peter S. "Striking Back for Tobacco." *Washington Post* (August 23, 1986), p. D1.

Carelli, Richard. "Court Lets Stand Iowa Restriction on Televised Lawyer Advertising." AP Wire (April 21, 1986).

————. "Court Will Study Lawyers' Ads Case from Kentucky." AP Wire (October 5, 1987).

Childress, Steven Alan. "Commercial Speech Doctrine under the First Amendment." *UWLAL Review* (Spring 1981), pp. 297-305.

Cohen, Richard. "Yes, Ban Cigarette Ads." *Washington Post* (August 15, 1986), p. A17.

Cohen, Dorothy. "Advertising and the First Amendment." *Journal of Marketing* (July 1978), pp. 59-68.

Colford, Steven W. "Rehnquist Slams Ads' 1st Amendment Shield." *Advertising Age* (June 30, 1986), p. 12.

"Constitutional Law-Commercial Speech Doctrine." *BYU Law Review* (1975), pp. 797-811.

Di Lullo, Samuel A. "The Present Status of Commercial Speech." *Dickinson Law Review* (Summer 1986), pp. 705-30.

Dingeman, Daniel J. "Constitutional and Statutory Regulation of Commercial Speech." *Michigan Corporate Finance & Business Law Journal* (Fall 1985), pp. 99-109.

Etheridge, Cynthia C. "Constitutional Law—Commercial Speech." *Mississippi Law Journal* (June 1984), pp. 319-37.

"Fairness and Unfairness in Television Product Advertising." *National Law Review* (January 1987), pp. 498-550.

Farber, Daniel A. "Commercial Speech and First Amendment Theory." *Corporate Practice Commentator* (Spring 1980), pp. 68-117.

Feldman, Michael. "Survey of the Literature: Commercial Speech." *Cardozo Law Review* (Spring 1981), pp. 659-97.

Fleuchaus, Jonathan. "First Amendment Protection for Commercial Speech." *University of Florida Law Review* (Summer 1979), pp. 799-814.

Foley, Adrian. "FTC Staff Sparks Debate." *Legal Times* (February 9, 1987), p. 12.

"Freedom of Speech, Press and Association." *Harvard Law Review* (November 1977), pp. 188-214.

"Free Speech Gets Fuzzier." *Los Angeles Times* (July 4, 1986), pt. 2, p. 4.

French, Thomas A. "Constitutional Law—First Amendment—Commercial and Non-commercial Speech." *Duquesne Law Review* (Summer 1982), pp. 637-68.

Friedland, Sandra. "State Board's Advertising Rules." *New York Times* (October 5, 1986), sec. 11NJ, p. 8.

Fuchsberg, Jacob D. "Commercial Speech: Where It's at." *Brooklyn Law Review* (Spring 1980), pp. 389-99.

Garrison, Michael J. "Should All Cigarette Advertising Be Banned?" *American Business Law Journal* 25 (Summer 1987), pp. 169-205.

Hankin, Janet S. "Constitutional Law—Commercial Speech." *University of Baltimore Law Review* (Winter 1985), pp. 367-79.

Heath, Julie E. "Attorney Advertising and Commercial Speech." *Tulsa Law Journal* (Spring 1986), pp. 591-609.

Hegarty, Michael. "Constitutional Law—First Amendment Commercial Speech." *University of Kansas Law Review* (Fall 1985), pp. 191-216.

Hovland, Roxanne. "The Future of Alcoholic Beverage Advertising." *Communications & the Law* 9 (April 1987), pp. 5-14.

"The Issue of Issue Ads." *Public Relations Journal* (October 1986), p. 20.

Jackson, Thomas H. "Commercial Speech: Economic Due Process and the First Amendment." *Virginia Law Review* (February 1979), pp. 1-41.

Kaplan, Marilyn R. "Commercial Speech and the Right to Privacy." *Columbia Journal of Law & Social Problems* (Spring 1980), pp. 277-315.

Kent, Felix. "Advertising and Free Speech." *New York Law Journal* (September 26, 1986), p. 1.

Kirkpatrick, James J. "How Much Freedom of Commercial Speech." *Courier-Journal* (December 21, 1985), p. 90E.

Klaidman, Stephen. "Cigarette Ads and Your Civil Liberties." *New York Times* (August 2, 1986).

Kurland, Philip B. "Posadas de Puerto Rico v. Tourism Company." *Supreme Court Review* (1986), pp. 1-17.

Kurnit, Richard. "First Amendment Protection for Commercial Speech." *New York Law Journal* (June 17, 1985), p. 1.

Labaton, Stephen. "Business and the Law: Speech Rights of Companies." *New York Times* (October 19, 1987), sec. D, p. 2.

"The Legacy of the Burger Court." *U.S. News & World Report* (June 30, 1986), p. 48.

Lynn, Barry W. "Outlawing Tobacco Advertising Is Not a Proper Remedy." *Los Angeles Times* (July 25, 1986), pt. 2, p. 5.

McChesney, Fred S. "Commercial Speech in the Professions." *University of Pennsylvania Law Review* (December 1985), pp. 45-119.

Manne, Henry G. "The Inversion of Constitutionalism (Canada)." *University of Toronto Law Journal* 37 (Summer 1987), pp. 260-67.

Marcus, Ruth. "ABA Rejects Prohibition of Tobacco Advertising: 'Censorship is Contagious,' Lawyer Warns." *Washington Post* (February 17, 1987), p. A6.

Maute, Judith L. "Scrutinizing Lawyer Advertising and Solicitation Rules under Commercial Speech and Antitrust Doctrine." *Hastings Constitutional Law Quarterly* 13 (Spring 1986), pp. 487-535.

Mercurio, James P. "Commercial Speech: Court Takes Step Backwards." *Legal Times* (July 28, 1986), p. 4.

Merrill, Thomas. "First Amendment Protection for Commercial Advertising." *University of Chicago Law Review* (Fall 1976), pp. 205-54.

Meyerowitz, Steven A. "The New Threat to Advertising Freedom." *Business Marketing* (October 1986), pp. 20, 22.

————. "When Privacy Goes Public in Advertising." *Business Marketing* 72 (March 1987), pp. 104-9.

Middleton, Kent. "Commercial Speech and the First Amendment." Ph.D. diss., University of Minnesota, 1977.

Miller, Matthew L. "Sam May Not Play It Again." *New York Times*, sec. 4, p. 23 (January 25, 1987).

Myers, Matthew. "R. J. Reynolds vs. the Government." *New York Times* (July 6, 1986), sec. 3, p. 2.

Neuborne, Burt. "A Rationale for Protecting and Regulating Commercial Speech." *Brooklyn Law Review* (Spring 1980), pp. 437-62.

Nienow, Thomas H. "The Common Sense Distinction between Commercial and Noncommercial Speech." *Hastings Constitutional Law Quarterly* 14 (Summer 1987), pp. 869-87.

Norton, Robert E. "Reagan's Imprint on the Courts." *Time* (November 24, 1986), p. 121.

Piercey, Dennis. "Legislative Choice and Commercial Speech." *Utah Law Review* (Fall 1981), pp. 831-42.

Plevan, Kenneth A. "Recent Decisions by Supreme Court Offer Commercial Speech Guidance." *National Law Journal* (October 21, 1985), p. 17.

Redmond, Suzan M. "Constitutional Law—Commercial Speech." *Texas Tech. Law Review* (Spring 1980), pp. 717-27.

"Rep. Synar Introduces Bill to Ban All Tobacco Ads and Promotions." *Daily Report for Executives* (February 19, 1987), p. A6.

Rome, Edwin P. "Bellotti and the First Amendment." *Corporation Law Review* (Winter 1980), pp. 28-49.

Rotunda, Ronald D. "At the Center: The First Amendment Now Protects Commercial Speech." *Center Magazine* (May 1977), p. 32.

————. "The Constitutional Future of the Bill of Rights." *North Carolina Law Review* 65 (June 1987), pp. 917-34.

Rovner, Julie. "Anti-Smoking Forces Stoke Legislative Fires." *Congressional Quarterly* 44 (December 13, 1986), p. 3049.

Sack, Robert D. "Commercial Speech." *Federal Commission Law Journal* (September 1984), pp. 217-24.

"Scope of Protection for Commercial Speech." *Harvard Law Review* (November 1980), pp. 159-68.

Seigenthaler, John. "Advertising of Lawful Products Should Not Be Banned." Testimony before Subcommittee on Transportation, Tourism and Hazardous

Materials, Washington, D.C. (April 3, 1987). Executive Speaker, speech no. 2347 (November 1987).

"Should Cigarette Ads Be Outlawed?" New York Times (February 22, 1987), sec. 4, p. 9.

Sharpe, Robert J. "Commercial Expression and the Charter." University of Toronto Law Journal 37 (Summer 1987), pp. 229-59.

Simon, Todd F. "Defining Commercial Speech." New England Law Review (Spring 1985), pp. 215-45.

"Speech Protection for Ads Limited." Facts on File World News Digest (July 11, 1986), pp. 499-C3.

"The Supreme Court, 1979 Term: Scope of Protection for Commercial Speech." Harvard Law Review (November 1980), pp. 159-78.

"The Supreme Court, 1980 Term: Commercial Speech." Harvard Law Review (November 1981), pp. 211-21.

Swartz, Karl. "Constitutional Law—First Amendment—Protection of Commercial Speech." University of Kansas Law Review (Spring 1984), pp. 679-96.

Talmadge, Candace. "Judge Denies TRO in Delta Ads Case." Adweek (October 5, 1987).

Taylor, Stuart, Jr. "High Court, 5-4, Sharply Limits Constitutional Protection for Ads." New York Times (July 2, 1986), sec. A, p. 1.

Tilner, Mitchell C. "Government Compulsion of Corporate Speech." Santa Clara Law Review 27 (Summer 1987), pp. 485-513.

Walker, Jerome, Sr. "Views of the Chief Justice on Advertising." Editor & Publisher (February 14, 1987), sec. 1, p. 26.

Waterson, M. J. "A New Threat to the Freedom to Advertise." International Journal of Advertising (UK) 6 (July 1987), pp. 67-71.

Weinberg, Jonathan. "Constitutional Protection of Commercial Speech." Columbia Law Review (May 1982), pp. 720-50.

Welkowitz, David S. "The Posadas Adventure." New York Law Journal (September 5, 1986), p. 5.

_____. "Smoke in the Air: Commercial Speech and Broadcasting." Cardozo Law Review (Fall 1985), pp. 47-91.

Whelan, Margaret. "Common Sense and Commercial Speech." University of Pittsburgh Law Review 48 (Summer 1987), pp. 1121-50.

Will, George. "The Civil Libertarians Are Blowing Smoke." Washington Post (July 24, 1986), p. A23.

Wulger, Gregory T. "The Constitutional Rights of Puffery: Commercial Speech and the Cigarette Broadcast Advertising Ban." Federal Commission Law Journal (July 1984), pp. 1-25.

Index